The Book That Could ~~Not~~ Be Written

20 Years Experience of Lessons Learned for People Leaders

Robert Kiely

Limerick, Ireland

PARTRIDGE
A Penguin Random House Company

Library of Congress Control Number: 2015906462
ISBN: Softcover   978-1-4828-3136-8
               eBook   978-1-4828-3137-5

Print information available on the last page.

To order additional copies of this book, contact
Toll Free 800 101 2657 (Singapore)
Toll Free 1 800 81 7340 (Malaysia)
orders.singapore@partridgepublishing.com

www.partridgepublishing.com/singapore

Contents

Contents

Dedicated to my wife Nadia and son Ethan.

Preface

There were a number of reasons why I decided to write this book, firstly, I was always told that there was at least one book in each of us. This to me was like a challenge that I always felt at some point I would have to attempt. The other reason for writing this book was because when I first took up the huge task of people management, all those years ago, my company sent me on a 10 week high-level overview course. I will never forget what the course instructor said to me, I'm pretty sure he was addressing the whole class but it felt like he was talking directly to me, nevertheless it stuck in my head for the last 20 years. His opening comments were, "Folks there is no book for this, lots of books touch on various aspects of supervision or people management but none capture it all in one book". That sounded like a challenge to me and one that I knew someday, when I felt it was right, I would have to attempt. The purpose of this book is to try and capture in simple terms (and hopefully not referring to too many theories and gurus) as many elements as possible that you find in the day to day management of people. As much as possible I have tried to include some stories from my own experience and tried to make it easy and fun to read. The real life experience, "the unwritten elements" as it were, is often hard to capture and often avoided in books. I also did not want to try and create some "flavor of the month book" where I would promise you that in 10 weeks you will *"Know it all for 19.99 – order now!!"* There are small easy to read chapters that you can pick up and put down when you have 5 minutes in your busy life. Some leaders have oodles of years experience but I'm sure that even they will get a nugget or two from this book. As a sideline comment, my marketing budget isn't exactly Hollywood blockbuster movie size so if you know of anyone taking on a leadership role please recommend it if you found it useful! So from one normal leader to another I hope you find 'The book that couldn't be written' more than just useful, I hope you find it interesting, informative and enjoyable – if nothing else, at the very least it will help you sleep.

Acknowledgements

I would like to thank Nadia & Ethan for putting up with me while I wrote this book. I would also like to thank all the great mentors I have been lucky to have in my own career to date, your advice was always appreciated if not always taken ☺...

TAKE YOUR TIME

BULL IN A CHINA SHOP

1

So you've been waiting for your leader to give you the good news, it finally arrives and your new role is becoming clear to you! Sound right? Of course it does but along with the great news you may be apprehensive, have concerns and self-doubts as to the scope of the role and where your responsibilities begin and end. All of these are very natural feelings and thoughts when taking on a leadership role.

In my first role I had to wear a shirt and tie for the first time since school. I only knew the schoolboy knot and had to learn the Windsor knot over the weekend. I took my shirt straight out of the packet and wore it straight away. The senior leaders saw all the crease lines and I was the butt of many jokes that Monday morning. So above all else, on Day 1, remember to iron your shirt!

In my experience of starting new roles in new or current organizations there are really only two ways in which you can "arrive". The first is like a *Bull in a china shop, the second is the City bus tour.*

Bull in a china shop

I called the title of this chapter after this ways, although I'm not in any way recommending this particular method of arrival. The closest description

I can give to it is the "bull in a china shop" approach. The image of a real bull in a real china shop brings to mind images of extensive damage to the structure of the shop, in addition to the emotional well-being of everyone involved in the shop. Not to mention the irreparable damage caused by the bull to the shops profitability and stock. Visualize this and you will start to see that in your new role, you are entering a shop of your own that has rules both written and unwritten. There is the official organization and the unofficial organization. As an aside, if things can't get done through the official organization then the unofficial organization will kick in and bypass roadblocks of all kinds. Anyway, back to our shop, it needs to be viewed as a shop that was working and operational before you arrived, and should continue to do so once you take your place at the helm.

Of course you have a vision and ideas of ways to improve it (or you wouldn't have been promoted or have been offered the job). The key thing here is timing. You can arrive like someone from an American western complete with 6 shooter pistol and meet everyone by saying "there's a new sherriff in town". Just to clarify, this too is *not* a recommendation in case the sarcasm was lost! I've seen so many potential positive beginnings destroyed by this bull in a china shop approach.

Or the *second* way is you can take the city bus tour approach. The name as it suggests, means that you allow yourself to be shown around the shop to understand what's currently going on and like any intrepid explorer you take notes. Just like the city tour from the open top bus you will see good, potential and bad. Do not assume you know everything on day one. You need to take your time to see before passing judgments.

There are many things to consider when you arrive. The people that have been there for years before you got there. How are they feeling about your arrival? Are they delighted you're there? It is indeed possible that your arrival is like an amazing anticipated biblical event, but the likelihood is, that like the rest of us you arrive into your new role to a bag of mixed emotions waiting for you.

• Perhaps there is someone who was promised your job and through the jigs and the reels did not get it. They are likely to be less than delighted to see you.

• The culture of the department or organization that you are now going to be in charge of, how did it evolve?

• What are the norms?

• In what ways is it the same and in what ways is it different to what you're used to? Remember, you are bringing your perspective and cultural experiences with you and this may not be the norm in your new organisation's culture. This can cause a conflict as you may be expecting one outcome and the reality is you might end up getting another. "Pay for this and they give you that" scenario i.e. they were expecting Jesus and got Rambo instead.

- Are there optimistic folk that will help you bring about reform and change? They are, usually, the friendliest people in your new team.

- Who are your allies and who needs to be watched?

- There will also no doubt be members of the team trapped in that old chestnut—"fear of change". Someone once said "the initial inertia for change is status quo." Sometimes, the way things were was a happy place to be and now it's all about to change in their eyes and it may genuinely scare them.

- Your predecessor may have been some kind of superhero and now you have a tough act to follow, or you could be one of the first pioneers to live in this new land as a leader.

- They may not be used to taking direction because they always did it all themselves.

The above paragraph looks at both extremes, the reality will most likely be a mixed bag. As leaders it is important to know it is not always very good or very bad! Unless you're extremely lucky or extremely unlucky.

Take your time

So what can you do? Don't panic if you haven't thought about all of these factors. A heightened sense of your environment in the early days can compensate for what you may have missed. Take your time when you arrive. That's the key message of this chapter. **Take your time**. *"Easy for you to say"*, I here you say, *"You don't have a boss breathing down your neck expecting all these changes yesterday"*. This is when your metal is tested, do not bend to this pressure, most good bosses will understand that it's going to take you a while to find your feet, get to know your way around and start making an impact. If you don't have one of these bosses then provide regular updates on how you are doing, so they are aware of the challenges you are experiencing and they might even be able to help you with historic data or legacies that are impossible for you to know.

Listen

This brings me nicely to another key aspect of your arrival which is Listen. Listen! Listen! Listen! You have two ears and one mouth so you should listen twice as much as you talk. I would encourage all of you to take a lot of time having one to ones with your team and key stakeholders early on, they are anxious to have their time with you and it also shows that you respect them and that you value their opinions.

Ask them questions about what they see as the areas for improvements.

- What is important to them?

- What does the team do well?

- What is the team's Achilles heel?

- What would you like to see happen in the next 3 months?

- What is the big ticking time bomb in the area?

- What is morale like on a 1-10 scale? If you are getting a score of less than 4, you have some people issues to deal with before you start imposing your plans. Otherwise they will not care and will not embrace any changes.

Try and get some quick wins completed to demonstrate that you are a leader, true to your word and that you really do listen and act. By listening, you start to get a feel for the culture and the hot issues of the area that should be on your priority list. Discuss these hot areas as you find them with your boss to ensure you are all aligned on the priorities. But remember, they are still important to your team despite of where they sit on a bigger priority list so try and do them or at least strike up a balance.

Beware of trying to be a crowd pleaser or committing to things you cannot change. I believe the term is "false promises for cheap sensationalism." For example, if *lack of promotional activity* is a concern, you can't create new opportunities for everyone on your team on your own, but you can help them develop themselves to move closer towards achieving their goals. False promises undermine your reputation. When making decisions beware of the advice that you are given, don't always take it as gospel. Find out for yourself from a few sources or you may end up getting played, being a puppet for others' intentions.

So in Summary

- Take your time when you arrive, look around.

- Don't act too quickly.

- Be sure to listen to your entire team, meet with them individually.

- Understand your business.

- Get to know your people well and make time for them.

- Figure out what your future challenges are.

- Ensure you are keeping your boss informed of your findings and observations.

- Once you feel you have a handle on things, go present your plans and ensure you get buy in from everyone before blasting ahead.

Remember all that and you should be fine, but if you don't, listening well will save you.

STORY:

I had a boss once, who had been transferred from another area internally, he had a reputation for getting things done. The area that he came from was physically removed from our area and had developed a somewhat prickly culture, ripe with distrust and politics. I am happy to say ours was not. Also this area had been the Crown Jewels for a while and we were left to our own devices and had still gotten the job done with half the fuss, and half the support. Unfortunately this boss chose not to listen to our advice, as per the first chapter. And to make matters worse he had been energized by superiors who had a certain opinion about our area. The carnage began by him not asking for help from anyone, cancelling meetings, public floggings, meetings exploded and he changed them to suit his own needs without understanding their previous benefits. He refused to learn how things worked there before his arrival. While struggling to understand, tempers were high and quickly a reputation was formed. Probably the biggest issue was the not listening and believing in third parties opinions rather than finding out for himself. The result was a big mess which took a few months to sort out. The impact was that there was a much colder culture within the team. Not surprisingly, it became similar to where this boss had just come from. People will always try and recreate what they know or believe to work. I still can't help but feel a quieter, more collaborative approach could have had us performing to his expectations much earlier.

THE ANSWER IS TIME ITS

AS SIMPLE AS THAT

PUTTING PEOPLE FIRST

2 During your time as leader, it is an absolute certainty that you will encounter issues or problems that will force you to make tough decisions. A large number of these decisions may be between people and company. In the early days of appointment, you will possibly be carrying feelings of gratitude to the company for the opportunity that has been presented to you, but you might also be feeling a motivation to make the company better. These feelings, although normal, can be dangerous if you let them influence your decisions and allow them to guide you to make decisions based only on the fact that "you have a job to do, isn't that why you were promoted?" No! Remember it is people such as yourself that have played a huge part in making the company great, people like you and me are the backbone of every company.

People come to work not as programmed machines but as people who are "working to live". They have kids, an "other half', a household to deal with and everything that comes with life. Newsflash, whether we like it or not all this comes in through the front door of your business too. I'm sure there has been some Monday mornings before you were a leader that you didn't feel great too right? My point here is that you need to put people first. Now if I had a euro for every time I heard that statement at a Human Resource meeting, I could have retired by now. However there is real meaning in those words "put people first". "Great, got it!" I hear you say. So how do you do it?

Time

Unlike other books, I will give you the magic formula, normally at this point you would find a whole lot of theory filled with great concepts but haven't the first notion how to implement them. As I said in the beginning I am very practical in my approach to this book. The answer is *Time*. It's as simple as that. When Mary comes in and you can tell she is flustered or Bill who usually has a spring in his step is walking a little heavier than usual. Take the time to ask them how they are doing? Is everything ok? Maybe give Mary and Bill a lift by saying that you saw that report or work they did yesterday and it was really impressive. Of course, we are touching on the subject of recognition which is covered in a later chapter called "The spoils should be enjoyed." However when you take the time to talk and more importantly listen to your team, you will start to learn more about them and also what their life/career priorities are. A quick example, a married man that likes to spend a lot of time with his wife and newborn baby may not value overtime that much whereas the guy who just bought a new house might be delighted with the resulting extra cash. Without taking the time to get to know your team, you could have ended up in an awkward situation where you ask the father of the new baby to work overtime and he ends up resenting you for it, whereas two meters away there was a guy who you may have motivated by giving him the overtime. So you see by knowing people you give yourself an advantage especially when you are forced to make decisions involving both the business and people. Another important point is that you should always seek the best option for the person involved and if it can be avoided, never make a decision that will have an impact on your team's morale. Yes, people are resilient, but remember you will have to work with these folks on other projects, maybe in other companies in the future. It's important to keep them motivated and to preserve the relationships between you and your people.

Win/Win

When a difficult decision comes along that implicates the people, the process and the business, aim for a win-win. This is the best option for both parties. Win/lose is easy, a trained monkey could probably come up with a solution for that. You are being paid to come up with a win/win solution.

Remember too that this problem should not be exclusively yours. You shouldn't have to retire to a mountain top and stare at a valley looking for inspiration and hoping to be hit with a bolt of lightning like some thought/decision scene in a movie.

A very effective approach that I have used is involving everyone (maybe everyone is a bit extreme?) or as many people as is practical in the problem. You will be pleasantly surprised by the outcome. State the problem and the dilemma you find yourselves in. Be sure to say the dilemma that WE are in, not that you are in. This shows involvement and reiterates the old saying "a problem shared is a problem halved." In a lot of cases you will find that a solution comes to the top quite quickly. Once a solution is agreed, check if everyone is ok with the proposed solution, or if they have any questions or concerns. By doing this, you have also increased trust with your team and they now see you as person that shares information with them. You have increased mutual respect as they now see that you value their opinions and the solutions that they bring to the table. They are also 'bought in' to the solution because they have been involved in coming up with the plan, and are therefore more likely to execute it than if you had issued a decree. Nobody expects you to have all the answers, but between your team and yourself, you will certainly have a lot of them.

Sometimes (particularly at the start of a new role and new team) you might feel that you are relinquishing your power as their leader by doing this but as I have demonstrated the reverse is actually true. You might have thoughts that your team see you as useless and are thinking that "all he does is call us in whenever he can't solve a problem". Thankfully, this is all in your head. Your job is to make the best decision and the best decisions are informed decisions.

The title of this chapter was 'Putting people first' so by talking to them, noticing their mood, asking how are they doing, supporting them, involving them when you need to make a controversial decision that effects them, you will succeed. Above all, remembering to put people first when there are smaller decisions to be made too and making time for them through regular 1 to 1's. I have dedicated a few words to 1 to 1's in another chapter called "mano a mano."

Humanity

A very powerful question is to ask "how do you feel about that?" and direct it at a specific individual if you feel they are not entirely on board with you or to the group in general to look for feedback. Try and outline what it is you are trying to achieve at the start and communicate clearly why you need their help/support. Once people feel they are on the journey with you it won't feel so lonely at the top and also will become quite enjoyable to work together through the good and bad times. Remember to treat people with respect at all times even if they have let you down, we are all human after all. Once you see the humanity in people and hold it high as a priority, your team will happily take direction from you, trust and confide in you and most importantly will come to you if they need help or assistance. Then you know you are truly putting people first.

STORY:

There was a factory that I worked in once that was extremely busy and the pressure was always on for meeting the build plan. The boss in question was a brilliant man but not of Irish origin. It was March and as bad luck would have it, March had fewer working days available than other months due to St Patrick's Day. So I remember being called to the boss's office to discuss production numbers and it became quite apparent that we were in trouble for making the month end figures. Knowing the boss like I did, I could quickly see where we were going to end up and what question I was going to be asked. The question would become a miracle of biblical proportions if I was going to be able to make it happen. Before I tell you what it was you must understand the culture of the team at the time. Busy busy busy. Long shifts and overtime were all commonplace. Milestone after milestone. Corporate pressure to increase numbers due to public demand and huge sales. People were tired and almost at breaking point. Tempers were short and the whole factory was on edge.

The title of a later chapter is "the air we breathe", which looks at culture. The understanding of what is around us, feelings emotions etc. By knowing this we can make better decisions and keep people first. It is also part of the culture to understand your Boss. This boss would not take no for an answer I can tell you and would argue in a very simplistic way and say. "It needs to be done".

The question was "Can we work St. Patrick's Day?"

I don't think I need to convey my surprise and shock all rolled into one. Our national holiday being asked to be sacrificed with an expectation of 100% turnout from everyone. Sometimes being a leader is difficult. I was faced with that question and would have to face my own team with it knowing I would be receiving laughter mixed with anger as the response. I think the boss here did not fully understand the culture and that the decision could have had consequences for the future and morale of the teams. There will be many situations like that but you must weigh up the impact and remember as much as possible to put the People first.

FOLLOW YOUR SCHEDULE
TO THE LETTER

THE ART OF JUGGLING

3   I'm afraid, the bad news is that there is no escaping the daily battle between what is deemed important and what is not? The good news is that there is an answer. When you look at your priority items it is important to realize that a number of factors influence the item. Pressure from above, missing a deadline, it has been deprioritized for too long and now it's late, your boss thinks its important etc. I could be here for hours listing the reasons. The key message here is that there is a reason why it is a priority. What I would say to you today is, that you need to understand fully why it is a priority? A lot of what I am saying here links closely to the later chapter called "time is precious" which deals with the importance of time management. You must understand each of the priorities, then take a ride in your helicopter and look down on them all together in order to see the big picture. No it's not crazy; this will give you a perspective from a business point of view of what's really important now and what can wait. One thing for sure is, that most of the time you can't get everything done in that day. If you try to, you will end up working late. Great plan. NOT. As you'll end up taking that mindset every day and work late every day.

On any given day each priority will feel like it's the hottest thing ever. The more information you gather on each priority the better. Things like background stuff, such as

- Is it a must have, or a nice to have?

- Where is the pressure coming from?

- Can it wait until tomorrow or is it really needed today?

- What is the real impact of not completing this today?

There is often huge pressure associated with priorities. So an effective way to relieve this pressure is to agree the priority list with your boss, especially if you're not sure. Write down all the items/tasks to be completed and grade them 1-15 in order of what you feel is the most important. This can take 5 minutes in the morning and it will be the best 5 minutes you will ever spend. Run the list by your boss and ensure that you are both in agreement. Now all that's left is to slot them in to your schedule and then "follow your schedule to the letter" beware of time wasters as this will mess up your schedule. Politely try and get a quick overview of the issue and try to ask them to schedule some time with you where you can devote your full attention. (Unless of course it looks like it is an important issue or personal issue from a team member or peer that they need your time). A maybe somewhat obvious point is that you should always give attention to what your boss deems a priority. Many reasons for this but the most important one is that he may have a different perspective at a higher level of what's needed in the company right now. Your focus will tend to be on the things that matter to you and your team. This does not mean that your priorities are in any way less important but you may not have the full picture that your boss has. Also don't be afraid to disagree if the priority ranking is changed by your boss. Seek to understand why it is more important and have the discussion if you feel strongly for why you had given the item more priority (this will also help you early on to see what company priorities are to the company.)

Disagree and Commit

In the end if you don't get your way you should apply a technique called disagree and commit. What's that? Well "disagree and commit" is where you acknowledge that you are both coming from different places in terms of the way forward or priority discussion but you realize that a decision has to be made or already has been made. You may disagree with the direction but you commit to support it. You can't win them all and it is not worth damaging the relationship with your boss, in addition pig-headedness is not an admirable trait in any leader. Once you have stated your position you can commit to implementing the request and be seen to be supporting it, not walking out of the office and bad mouthing the decision. You are now management and must be seen, at all times, to be a leader. This is not always easy to do especially if the passion is there for a given direction and it has not happened but your day will come. The main thing is to realize that your opinion is valued or you wouldn't be in the room.

When you are in the big chair you will have to make the big decisions too and you not eve ryone will agree with you either. If they do agree all of the time, then you're on a different planet or you are surrounded by 'yes men'. These are the type of people that are like those dogs in the back window of cars that bob their heads up and down, whatever the boss says they just go "YES". My advice is to have your own voice and listen to all angles.

There is no getting away from the fact that priorities are difficult to handle and they will challenge you every day. So understand them all in their entirety as best you can. Take a step back and look at them from 50,000ft up in the helicopter, the view is different up there will help you to see what you think is the reason it has become a priority, make your decision and if you're not sure seek agreement from your boss.

One key point to remember, especially when it comes to decisions involving people, is that you are closer to the action than your boss. For all intents and purposes, you are like a gauge or a device to measure the heat of the situation. Don't be afraid to trust your gut if you feel an issue is at boiling point and your boss doesn't feel the same way. You are feeling all the emotions, you see all the potential risks etc. So speak up if you feel something is like a ticking time bomb.

Be aware also that because you have been bombarded with emotions by your subordinates or peers on a certain item you may be biased and influenced by their emotions. So check yourself, see if you are supercharged, look objectively at the decision and ask yourself what is influencing you. It's nice to be a leader and stand up for your team but you are now management and also need to see the business perspective equally. An example might be a priority shipment or task that may require overtime on a holiday weekend for example. You are feeling the emotions of your team not to work the weekend and are ready to challenge your boss. However stop and check the reasons for the request, see if it makes business sense and the big picture before you go flying the flag of freedom. When thinking about this chapter I visualized the concept of the circus and a juggling clown performing. As a leader you will be required to juggle all the balls in the air at once. Giving them all attention frequently. I have even seen acts where multiple items are juggled and plates are balanced on sticks while juggling. This image can be very accurate for your day to day and week to week juggling of your priorities. A good way to balance this is by having good forums for everything to be discussed (all the balls in the air at once) so that frequent attention is given to all aspects. If it doesn't have a forum to be discussed daily/weekly it doesn't get managed.

STORY:

I was doing some consulting once and was asked to take a look at a manufacturing area that was losing money. At first I could see really high energy and positive culture. Willingness to do the right thing and get better and fantastic commitment to customer. It all sounds great right, so what was I missing? Yes they were juggling all the balls but with one or 2 people who of course dropped a few now and then. What I did was put some structure in place. Good meetings with focused agendas. Good structure with roles and responsibilities clearly defined. Everyone knew where we were going because the vision and business updates were shared weekly/ daily. The leaders became leaders with visions and not firemen responding to the latest fire. Every priority that was raised had a forum where it could be discussed and actioned. What started out as an under 8yr old kids rugby game, where they all follow the ball with no structure and one goal on their mind – to get the ball - was transformed into a Swiss clock that felt confident in addressing any new issue and rose to every challenge and began to self-improve.

So have meetings or forums to remove the balls from the air and give them a home. It's easier to juggle one ball. The rest get put onto an agenda and get discussed in a team forum. As a general rule you should have no more than 4-6 key meetings with your team every week to cover all the balls and don't forget to add or remove new tasks as and when necessary.

THE PERSPECTIVE OF YOUR
BOSS IS IMPORTANT

BRIDGE OVER TROUBLED WATER

4 In the context of the theme of this book, this title might strike you as a bit odd. Why is this chapter included in here? This isn't going to help me with managing my priorities, getting the best out of my team etc. Well you're right and wrong. Certainly at the start of your management career you can't really see its importance but as you grow into your role you will recognize that it is essential.

The perspective of your boss is important. If you think your boss is doing something just to get up your nose then that's probably not a good place to start. Mind you some bosses are experts at getting up peoples noses. In the middle of the madness that is the life of a Leader you will sometimes get the call that something has become a priority and needs to be done right away. This brings with it a great deal of stress and messes up your day and your schedule. Often the immediate emotion felt is anger and frustration or maybe you're totally in control of your feelings, well done if you are. For the rest of us, this insertion of panic into our day can cause problems. The common reaction would be for us to react in one of the following ways, either

- defer the request,

- dismiss it,

- don't bother with it

- Think to hell with him "Doesn't he realize how busy I am?"

- Or "I have no time for that"

A more centered view or objective view would be to ask, why are they asking me to do that? The most likely explanation is that it has become your boss's priority and therefore it is now your priority. You are left with the task of trying to figure this out on top of the current days' workload. But hey! It's part of our job right?

Depending on how new you are to your position, there is often an inner pressure of expectation that we set on ourselves at the start to ensure we complete every task and nothing is left for tomorrow. As we mature into the role we realize that that is not always possible thanks to there being only 24hrs in one day. We can do some things here to lighten the load a bit and help build a relationship with your boss. A good way is to ask your boss to sit with you for a few minutes while you go through your schedule, prioritize together what's important for your day, and move out the rest. This is a very simple but very effective tool. Your first reaction to this is probably one of *"Are you crazy? My boss will think I'm stupid if I ask them that"*. But actually, your boss should be happy to do that as now they will know that you are definitely going to work on what's important for them.

You are also doing something else when you do this regularly, building a relationship bridge. Try to set up a regular meeting in the morning to do this exercise with your boss. Your boss will have priorities and so will you. The ones that are important are your bosses, they get the 51% share. Why do I say that? Well if you put yourself in their shoes they only have you reporting to them you have the majority of the work force. Their main avenue for getting things done is through you. You are so important in their plans and you probably don't even realize it. So if you are in your boss's shoes and your boss says this item is hot and needs doing, you only have one option and that is to ask the leader of the majority of people (YOU) to complete it. So if you decide not to do this, you potentially end up making your boss look bad. If this happens then you are potentially damaging your reputation as an excellent completer/finisher. This bad situation (you and your boss look bad) that I have outlined can happen when you have a new leader in a role and they get what I call "superman syndrome," they rush to do everything that is thrown at them and never consult their boss and expect their teams to share the burden without any structure or forums being used. All they are missing in their own minds are capes and alter egos.

However if you consult with your boss you will understand their priorities and also begin to build up a relationship. You will start to see patterns emerge of what is important to your boss. What puts them at ease, what they hold sacred, what are their pet hates. Your goal is to make your boss feel at ease. The only way for this in the early stages is frequent communication. Give regular updates on tasks that have been deemed a priority. Make them feel comfortable that it is being worked on and also if possible say when it will be completed. Always allow yourself a little flexibility here. This is not being dishonest but it is being fair to allow for Murphy. Murphy's law for anyone that has lived under a rock is "anything that can go wrong will go wrong" this is a bit negative I agree but in operations or any process involving a lot of human interaction things can and will go wrong e.g. Communications didn't happen, people were out sick etc. So always allow a bit of leeway. Add it on at the end, as you are closer to the action you need to protect your boss too. As he will be using the information that you have provided to update their boss, it better be right. The upside is if you are early then you look like a hero (rarely happens). I knew guys that would do this to look like heroes (hero syndrome) if a job took an hour they would say 3 and finish in 2 quite comfortably and look like heroes. I don't condone this behavior because it's not in the best interests of the culture, people or the business. They get the job done but at what expense? Sooner or later these guys get found out through time and motion studies or LEAN operations or Kaizen events.

By getting to know your bosses preferences and priorities you also start to gain an insight into the next level of management and get the bigger picture for yourself. This allows you to prioritize more effectively when you start to learn what can wait until tomorrow and what can't. You are then essentially maturing into your role. A word of caution here. If your boss changes then you may be back to the beginning like snakes and ladders. Your new boss may hold different things sacred. Don't assume your old bosses priorities are the same as your new bosses priorities or values. A lot of people have left companies for that very reason. All you have to do is go back to the start and ask them for input into prioritizing your schedule and start again. You may not agree with the new boss and maybe you can engage in some positive discussion around why you disagree but too much of this in the early stages can be seen as defiance by your boss and it unsettles them a bit. The worst thing you hear as a leader of a new area is "why *are we doing it that way we always used to do it this way?* It just comes across as resistance to change. Mind you a clever boss should investigate the merits of existing processes before changing them. However as we all know some bosses arrive with a bang and some blend in slowly.

Being Nice, Being Human

Experiment with niceness and a friendly approach, remember your boss the iron, masked character that breathes fire and can crush buildings with their thumbs is actually a human being just like you. Try at the frequent meetings to ask about the kids or what their weekend plans are. Small stuff. Hopefully they grow to confide in you and run stuff by you. This is where you want to be as then you understand them fully and you understand the business needs fully. You are now fully informed and able to make the best decisions for your business and your career.

I called this chapter Bridge over troubled water, I am conscious that it may have similarities to the last chapter but it would not be honest of me to write a book that was all great and smelling of roses. Sometimes in life you will have negative bosses and you will need to know how to deal with them and survive...

STORY:

I had a boss once who had a collaborative style and left you manage your area and your team. Shared the goals and trusted me and the team to deliver. Holidays were okay as long as we had cover arranged and communicated we would be out etc. It was a pleasure to come to work and I enjoyed every day. The boss was like our Parents and they looked after us and we always had an ear to talk to them. Unfortunately this Boss was moved on and a new one took their place who wanted a process for everything, holiday schedules with rules of how many could be off on any given day. Zero flexibility for the team and a micro-managing style that made everyone uneasy. Nobody felt comfortable to go to them in times of trouble or if they were in need of guidance. The result was that absenteeism went up, attrition went up, as did tempers. The culture changed and as a result the team's motivation went to zero. Orders and deliveries were missed. Nobody cared anymore. The more the new boss shouted the less they listened and so the downward spiral commenced. I am a lot older now and I can see that the order and structure they were trying to implement was fine but they never involved the group in the so called "improvements" The result was that they appeared as threats to the team. They found it difficult to see the positives in the improvements and structure because they had not been told. If you want to instigate change bring your team with you and involve them.

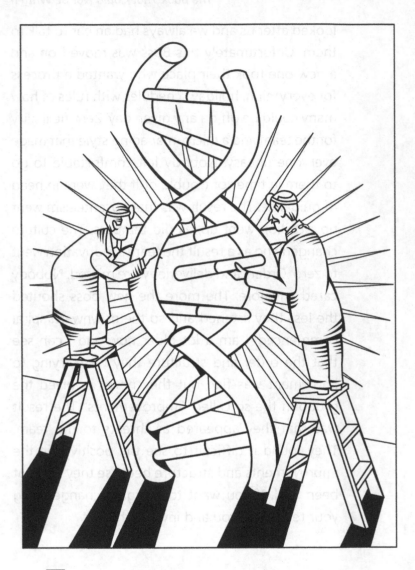

THIS IS ONE OF THE MOST IMPORTANT THINGS YOU WILL DO AS A LEADER

MANO A MANO

5 When I first encountered the phenomenon that is the "one to one" I have to be honest, I was less than convinced. The Idea of being all alone in a room talking about someone's performance was the equivalent feeling to walking blindfolded through a minefield. However I'll admit that I could not have been more wrong. It was a time where my own discomfort with the process was taking control and blinding me to the real benefits. As a new leader there will be a lot of new items that come along and some will come naturally and some will need work. Like learning a skill. This is one of the most important things you will ever do as a leader. Let me say that again ***this is one of the most important thing you will ever do as a leader.*** If you decide not to read any more of this book after this, I am ok with that as long as you really take this chapter and fully internalize it.

So after that introduction let's look at what this one to one process is all about. If I am to be honest it is a concept that has been around for at least 10-15 years at this stage. It is essentially a regular sit down with individuals from your team where you discuss their goals and performance and development. The traditional One to One would have been around seeing:

- How you fit in with the objectives?

- How are you achieving your goals?

- How are you getting on with your reporting metrics etc.?

It was your boss's way of keeping in touch with how you were getting on. It gave your boss a comfort feel as to how you were doing. It consisted of a private setting and there were guidelines associated with it. There was even a template that you had to complete with headings. Look for it. I am sure your company has it. Don't look too hard because what I will tell you now is that if your company has one. Throw it out. Do it spectacularly though. Role it in a ball and shoot some baskets into the corner trash bin in your office. As you can see I am a big fan of one to one templates (NOT). Hello!!! We are dealing with people. They don't fit into templates!!! The very concept of a template for this is ridiculous when you think of it.

Now in case I am not clear. The one to one is the most powerful force you will ever come across as a Leader, the element that I am not a fan of is overly structured one to ones. They make the Leader initiate most of the talking. The direct report finds themselves answering questions and talking about the business and taking actions which equate to more work for them. This is ok to a small extent.

After all we are in business, but don't forget what makes your business successful. PEOPLE.

One to Ones, by the way, at the start can seem very awkward and difficult. I know I struggled with them and wanted to be out of the room as fast as possible. It's like learning to ride a bike. It takes time. Don't try and be someone you're not. Be yourself. The most frustrating thing that I see about one to one's is the lack of personal contact between the two individuals there. Remember that if the person is not comfortable in themselves then they sure as hell aren't going to be focused on and care about how the business is going. Your job is to understand what is important to them, show them that you understand that, and are taking it on board. Really taking it on board, not just using the "I'll take it on board cliché". A really useful tip is understanding people's body language which I use a lot. It will tell you how engaged a person is on a given subject. Are they looking around the room? Are they sitting forward engaged with you? If you notice this stuff then call it out "I see you're really interested in this "or "is this stuff really boring? Understand them, that's why templates drive me crazy, anyone can complete a template but have you really connected with and motivated your team member. Imagine what they are saying when they leave the one to one. Is it *"thank god that's over for another month"* or is it? "That *was great my Boss really listened to me and my problems and we have a way forward together on this."* So be vigilant of the state of mind that the person is in. Try and get them when the madness has calmed down for a while. Timing is everything too, but I would insist that you are disciplined in ensuring that they occur religiously every month. Ask them to set up appointments in your calendar for their one to ones. In that way you have it and they have it. Now sometimes these will need to be rescheduled. Just as long as they are rescheduled and not forgotten about!

Content

Now in terms of content I have a few items that I think should be included. For me I want the result to be that I have a full understanding of what's going on in their lives and where their head is at. People are like icebergs. All you see is the 10% above the water. We have no idea what is going on in people's lives when they are not at work. Now I am not endorsing that you become a nosey parker but what I am saying is that people bring this stuff to work. Anyone who wants to think that people become robots as soon as they are in the building are kidding themselves. People are affected by events that occur outside of work. It is your job as a people leader to notice when people are not functioning well, when they look tired, annoyed, upset etc. Now this is a hard thing to do because you have meetings to go to etc. and you can't be holding their hands for the full day. That is why the one to ones become more important. And even at that the one to one is probably only once a month which may not capture all the items that occurred during the month in terms of how they have been feeling daily. Never fear, if you carry out a one to one which is primarily people focused then you will notice a spin off occurring. People begin to trust in you and are willing to share and approach you whenever they are in trouble. You have laid this foundation through your people focused one to one and as a result the direct report trusts you and feels comfortable to approach you for advice and support. Not all of these approaches will be work related in fact I put it to you that they will be mainly outside of work issues. If you remember in chapter one "putting people first" this is that entire message in action. This is your forum for starting to talk to your team and build relationships.

Now you may think there is a lot of digging and probing of individuals required to get to this "emotional stuff" however its quality not quantity. People generally want to talk about themselves and where they are. Your job is to notice and listen. Be aware of giving advice if you are not qualified to do so. Recommend that they seek help or direct them to Human resources if you feel you are out of your depth on a serious issue. If you have an employee support counseling service available recommend that. Avoid the "I'll tell you what you should do."

People in emotional states need support first and then advice later. Depending on the trauma the advice could be days later. Just let them know you are there for them and you understand what they are going through and offer them unconditional support from a work perspective as they could be worrying about missing time due to the issue. Sometimes it just takes a simple question *"are you ok?"* to open the flood gates.

So what kind of stuff do you include in the one to one? It's very simple really, you don't dictate the agenda. What? I hear you say. Yes, you go where they want to go (Remember we spectacularly threw away the one to one template so the agenda is gone too.) This is true for the majority of the one to ones. Just to ensure the job is getting done for the first 10 minutes go through the business stuff and then put it aside and simply ask "how are you doing?" and no, not like Joey in Friends. Their initial reaction might be that they go back into a work context and start speaking about the project, issue etc. If that happens, wait for them to finish and say politely, *"That's great but how are you doing, not work...how are things with you?* This might take them by surprise the first time you do this, but bear with it. And don't be discouraged if you don't get their innermost secrets on the first one to one. Remember this is essentially relationship building on a deeper level and relationships take time. And then the most important thing is to listen. If you are stuck for a good opener ask them to rate their current happiness level from 1 to 10. Where 1 is it's time to leave I am so out of here and 10 is I'm fully engaged smiling and having fun and being happy to be at work every day. (By the way if you meet a 10 send me on their name) most of us will be 7 or 8 tops. I am a realist and this is the most you can hope for. Great if you manage to get all your team to 10.

So in summary the one to ones are the best thing you can do and the best tool you have as a people leader. Be religious about having them, be yourself and be available at all times when your people have a problem. If you truly believe that people are number 1 then make them number 1. This means dropping everything when a member of your team has a problem and they come to you. Make time for them and cancel meetings if necessary. The one to one gives you a gauge as to how your people are doing and it gives you access to the real issues that are going on within the teams and also in their own lives. Also from a development point of view you gain an insight into where they are going career wise. And if you don't know? Ask them. By listening to them and working on these issues you gain their trust and also they feel more comfortable, like a weight has been lifted. Even if they don't say it they appreciate it. You might hear it back at a Christmas party or get together some time later.

STORY:

One of my first one to ones with an employee, I have to admit I couldn't honestly say who was more terrified—the employee or I. I was full of guidelines and procedure and focused on getting the desired outcome from the session. I was sadly devoting very little time to the individual and more to the One to One process and ensuring I was going to deliver an effective, productive one to one. At least I thought it was going to be productive. I had scheduled the appointment in the person's calendar and sure enough on time they turned up. I was all ready with my template and the name and date filled in at the top. The person came in and sat down and I was clinging to this template and ensuring I was following it and getting enough information for me to handwrite into the white boxes. I'd say I barely made eye contact with the individual. Onwards I went through line performance and focus areas as a team, gave feedback on performance data. Ask for help on process issues and when I had got to the bottom of my template I concluded the meeting and thanked the individual ensuring to get an agreed date scheduled a month from now for our next one to one. I was delighted with myself. "That wasn't so bad" I thought, "I can do this." A few days later I was in the canteen and a peer told me that my employee (the same one who had received a professional one to one) was about to hand in his notice. I was both shocked and confused. "How could he not have mentioned that at our one to one "I thought? I decided to follow up on the rumor and talk directly with the individual. I will never forget what happened then. He proceeded to tell me that the one to one was fine and he wanted to tell me about all the issues on the line and the staff morale and how he couldn't face another day in the place etc. etc. I never asked him about himself or gave him an opportunity to speak. It was business, business, business, and as delighted with myself as I was I had missed a fundamental part of what the one to one should be about. I felt ill, deflated and helpless all at the same time. All was not lost as we went for a coffee and I then listened to everything. He vowed to stay and we worked together to resolve the issues. The key message for me was to listen more than talk. Ask probing questions and ensure their wellbeing is ok.

HOW WE DO THINGS
AROUND HERE

THE AIR WE BREATHE

6

What is Corporate Culture? Let's look at the 2 words separately; corporate meaning large companies, mainly multi-nationals, big profits, big machines etc. Culture is what we experience every day the "how we do things around here". In order for these giants to function there has to be a consistency of approach no matter where in the world your segment of the business is. This can lead to a lot of policies that are trying to create a behavior that is workable and acceptable for their company. The culture can be fast paced or slow and compliant or anything in between. The better ones tend to have invested a lot of time and money in getting it right and ticking all the boxes to ensure employees are happy and motivated in their workplace. The not so good ones tend to ignore the people aspect and focus on the profits and the results is an entirely different culture. You can have a very people centered culture where people come first and the company takes a genuine interest in the well-being of its people. Or you can have a profit centered business which can tend to ignore the people until one of them breaks.

Some cultures like a lot of pre-thought before a project, some are more entrepreneurial and want a result with minimal thinking. In highly regulated cultures there is a focus on duty of care so things can appear to move slower. It's important to know what culture you are in as this can determine how you should function and operate. You may also need to adjust your style particularly if you are joining a new company. You will in time discover a culture that suits your work ethic and this will become an important factor when choosing a new Job. Following the best paid job offer might be good for your pocket but could be detrimental to your happiness and job satisfaction if the culture is not a fit for you.

Also remember we live in a small diverse world now and while some approaches will work with one ethnic group they may be alien to another. The western approach may not work in the east and vice versa. Try and understand the local culture where you are. The work ethic of the locality (career focused or transient). Try as they may the cultures themselves develop sub cultures. For example the way things are done in plant A vs. plant B. Even though they are the same company and have the same policies, they may not have the same culture. Reasons for this can be demographics, country cultures, different, management styles within the company, legislation for employees differs in different countries—some are very pro employee and some are more pro company. Company cultures and organization cultures can be grown and need to be closely monitored in the early years of the company as they are very difficult to undo later if they go wrong. There are hundreds of books on organizational culture and organizational structures, it is a subject in itself.

Awareness

My point from a front line leader's point of view is that awareness is key. It is vital that you are aware of the culture that you are in and most importantly that you understand its positives and its limitations. Promote its positives at all times with your teams and work to correct or improve the limitations where you can. The culture directly impacts the well-being feeling of your team. If they are unhappy because of something in the culture or policies then they may not perform to the required level and valuable time will be lost to productivity while they are discussing it amongst themselves. Sometimes you won't be able to do anything about policy changes that impact them but at the very least take a time out to acknowledge their concern and commit to working with the team to understand locally any concerns they have and commit to getting back to them. But **DO** get back to them or you will lose credibility. And if there is nothing you can do say exactly that, but explain the big picture if you can and show them what the company is trying to achieve by doing this. Do not sugar coat or make things up. If the company is downsizing say its downsizing for example, unless it's confidential of course. As a leader you are privy to confidential information that you otherwise might not be. People are smart they already know the reason before you speak with them.

Calmness

Work to ensure the culture is as calm as it can be, the calmer and more organized your team, the more routine and predictable they will become and less stressed. You can influence your own local culture as you are the leader. What is important to you will be important to them. The best cultures are ones that promote self-growth and continuous improvement as a norm. In that way, your group is constantly learning and improving and never standing still. Introduce bench marking to ensure the standards are high and keep trying to get there. Even the best cultural engines need to evolve.

STORY:

The single biggest awakening for me in terms of the impact of culture would have to be my time spent in China as a consultant. Arriving on a plane with a head full of western thinking. I had been asked to work closely with an operations team. A brilliant bunch of people with fantastic energy and a willingness to improve like I had never seen before. They were so enthusiastic taking all my experience and putting it all to work at an alarming speed. No committees, No lengthy reviews. Just implementation. I had to adapt my style initially to be very supportive and planting ideas / visions in their heads. Setting a vision and sharing it and allowing them to figure out the "how" and in so doing they were learning. People migration and attrition was different than Europe so models of productivity and line design for the first time in my career were now being influenced by culture. Ask an industrial engineer in Europe to factor in culture next time you meet one and see what response you get! I would say it would not even factor into the western thinking. Also leadership training had to be altered to suit the culture as I was the outsider coming in. Trust has to be earned first.

But from a European standpoint it is very apparent from company to company that company cultures are different. Choose where you want to work wisely and above all be sure that it suits your work ethic and style and if you find yourself in a culture you can't function in, then either adapt or possibly seek a more suitable culture for you.. Also remember that as a leader you contribute to the culture everyday by your decisions and your behaviors. These become norms and form a culture. If it's impossible to get a day off around here, it might have something to do with your holiday process or procedure because now we have a culture of hard work and no holidays forming. Your behavior directly influences the culture. Understand the consequences of your actions.

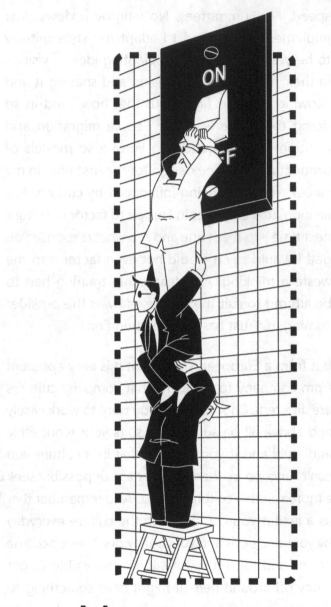

MANY HANDS MAKE
LIGHT WORK

YOU CAN'T DO IT ALL YOURSELF

7   For most of us the joyous days of promotion are
    filled with eternal possibilities some fear and maybe
    some self-doubt. All very natural I might add. What
    always amazes me is the self-driven expectations
    that newly promoted leaders place on themselves.
    As if their new role wasn't going to be challenging
    enough they decide to place additional pressures
    on themselves. Nobody has asked them to do this.
    I am talking about I suppose the ideals that we
    see in the new role. The "I'm going to change this,
    that, and that" approach. Again all very noble but
    I would seek clarity and direction from my new
    boss as to what he or she sees as the important
    elements to focus on in the new role. Despite this,
    new Leaders have their own personal tasks or
    change projects that they wish to impose. The plate
    can become very full very quick. I cannot stress
    enough the need to retain your first impressions
    of a place or the areas for improvement that you
    see need attention. There is nothing to say that all
    these improvements need to be completed ASAP.
    Write them down somewhere and revisit them in
    to 6 months. It is said that after 6 months in a
    role we become institutionalized. Meaning that you
    become part of the status quo and cannot see the
    areas for improvement and you become part of
    the system. In the early months be aware of this

and draw comparisons from previous jobs or areas, what worked well there, what is good here, what needs improvements here etc.

The next thing to realize 'you can't do it all yourself. Never a truer word has been spoken. Your responsibilities depending on the organization and the culture can range from safety of your team to ensuring you have attendance at canteen improvement meeting. Smaller organizations tend to expect more from their leaders. You are the be all and end all when it comes to everyone's solution for the problem. "Contact the manager." If I had a cent for every time I heard those words either written in a policy or uttered at a meeting as a fix for a problem I would be a wealthy man. Everyone expects you to be all seeing and all knowing. The all Seeing Eye comes to mind. This expectation that others place on you is very infectious and can cause you to believe that you need to be like this. I say that it's physically impossible for you to be everywhere, seeing everything and feeling everyone's feelings simultaneously. The very thought is insane and yet we have all felt this expectation of us. Not to be totally damning of this expectation, there is an element of truth in it. You are expected to know what's going on in your area, but you're not expected to have to physically go and do everything. You were promoted for a reason. The powers in your head, the knowledge you have acquired are now all in play.

So how do you achieve this all seeing all knowing position? There is a belief that the more you rise in an organization the more time you need to be working "ON" the business and less time "IN" the business. What this means is that you should spend more time reviewing the business and trying to improve it rather than being right in the thick of the action. This is now your new role to evaluate data, review errors and challenge fixes to ensure they are long-term. Sharing the power of your vision.

Believe in the power of your team.

Now forgive the sports analogy but like a football team you need to know every individuals skills and what they bring to the game. Similarly your team has hidden skills that you don't know about and you need to understand them as best you can. Imagine if you had some work to do and you needed some help, you know a certain member of your team is really interested in that area and would be happy to help. Everyone's happy, you have a good person on a particular piece of work the individual is motivated and developed and feels an involved part of the team etc. The benefits are huge and remember not all benefits are always visible to you.

Now contrast that with not knowing your team and randomly picking people for tasks, you may pick the best person or you may not, you don't know whether the person you picked or their neighbor is better at doing it and you will never know. Now the person selected feels obliged to help and maybe won't say no or recommend someone else because you're new and they don't know you. The better candidate for the work feels demotivated because you have not noticed them and they may possibly be jealous of their colleague who was selected.

Span of Control

The first thing to do is understand your span of control – another buzz term for what you are responsible for and what you can influence. The second thing is through your one to ones you should gain an understanding of where your team's individual interests lie. Take time to ask them in the one to one however don't use the dreaded line "where do you see yourself in 5 years" I cringe when I hear it. When you have a grasp of where your team is going you can try and best match their needs with the projects and work that present themselves from time to time and in fact the routine tasks also. You are helping their development (although they might not think so) and you are also working towards the all seeing all knowing expectation without the stress.

There are only 2 types of knowledge in the world, knowledge you have and knowledge you know where to get. Do not think that you must have all the worlds' answers for your department on the tip of your tongue. (Great if you can). You need to know where to get it most of the time and follow up with the requestor. The realization of this can relieve a lot of stress too. Beware of others preconceived expectations of you. Your goals and objectives set by your boss and the requests of you from your team are the most important things to be focusing on. If you can do the others great and no wonder you got promoted! Once you understand the skills of your team invite those to help you with your workload it could be as simple as gathering information for a weekly report or as complex as a major project. Knowing your team's skills will help you to delegate more easily. Delegation itself is about clear expectation setting and ensuring the receiver has received the message you gave complete with deadlines. Understand the individual capability of the person and assign projects / tasks correctly based on complexity and capability of the person. "Many hands make light work" as the saying goes but you are doing a development action and sharing business knowledge at the same time. This allows you more of that working "ON" the business time that we spoke about earlier. The vision setting and direction setting that leaders are supposed to be doing but sometimes gets lost while you are in the war trenches. Take time to stick your head up and look around by using your team to help you.

Robert Kiely

STORY: The Wolf and the Shepherd

A wolf had been prowling around a flock of sheep
for a long time, and the shepherd watched very
anxiously to prevent him from carrying off a lamb.
But the wolf did not try to do any harm. Instead
he seemed to be helping the shepherd take care
of the sheep. At last the shepherd got so used to
seeing the wolf about that he forgot how wicked
he could be.

One day he even went so far as to leave his flock
in the wolf's care while he went on an errand. But
when he came back and saw how many of the
flock had been killed and carried off, he knew how
foolish to trust a wolf as he exclaimed. "I have been
rightly served; why did I trust my sheep to a wolf?"

Moral: Delegate your task wisely, and only to people you trust.

YOU NEED TO RETAIN
WHO YOU ARE AND NOT
PUT ON A COSTUME

GOLDEN INGREDIENTS

8 When you are first promoted to a position where you are no longer depending on yourself to achieve, but now you need to achieve through others. Hmmn, this can be pretty daunting to say the least. You may have been promoted from within the team or from another department or hired new into the company. Each route to promotion holds their own strengths and weaknesses. Let's take a minute to look at these. It is important to know your strengths and weaknesses in your new role. A good tip is to take time out to understand them before you start. Knowing what you are bringing to the table and what you will need to work on is a crucial component of your future team. Whatever areas for improvement you personally have you may want to compensate by having someone that can assist in that area on your team. For example if finance was an area you were weak on be sure to have a strong finance person on your team or build in a link to one to review your data on a weekly basis etc.

The person promoted internally

On the positive side, the person promoted internally has all the knowledge of the process or area that they now have responsibility for. They are not going to be fooled or blindsided by excuses as they have seen it all and probably developed a piece of the area during their years of service there. This strength is great as you will continue to be the go-to person for all problems and at the big meetings you will be the one the senior staff asks for help when it gets too detailed for them. You will also hold the power of quick decision making and know what technical or information calls to make quickly.

On the flip side, you may have difficulties now asking or directing folks to do work who up to last week you were having lunch with and discussing their kids and holiday plans. Now you are their boss. They may view you differently now. Be aware of this. I don't know if it's an expectation we have ourselves or if it is told to us that you must become distant or a transformer and become a different person now that you are the boss. I think that there are new and important conversations to be had in starting the new relationships (one to ones we have already covered in this book)... Unfortunately we do and have all seen the transformers. Friday they are given the news and spend all weekend shopping for the new suit that's on full display at work on Monday morning.. Oh yes and by the way I was one of the transformers. My point (eventually) is that there is no way that a cheap suit and a bad tie can change who I am over the course of a weekend.

You need to retain who you are and not put on a costume. You will need to develop your own leadership style that best suits your personality. How do I do that? I hear you say. Well I think you take the best bits from all the leaders you ever had and combine them to make your own leadership style the best version. Remember leaders lead by example, and your reports are watching you every second. No Pressure then right?

The leader hired externally

The leader hired from outside has a different role. They may have previous people management experience and may not have a clue of the current process of getting things done. They won't know their staff at all or who does what. In this position you can often feel quite vulnerable and when people look to you for answers you may feel stupid if you don't have them. You may also feel susceptible to being taken advantage of by your new team who may be testing you for the last minute holiday request for example. Or you may have to listen to the classic resistance to change statement "it was always done like that before you came" trying to make you feel insecure about rocking the boat. Don't forget this leader has experience already in the bag and just needs to learn the policies or process and they are off and running. You may feel the need to acquire knowledge of the process and don't want to ask the folks as that would make you look silly. My advice is to tell them you haven't come across it yet and it will take you time to understand it. Also ask them what would they recommend and if you don't have any concerns follow it by saying "I will support your decision," "as you guys know best right."

There is also the possibility that you got promoted from within the company but will be moved to a different area and department. This can be used to avoid the awkwardness of being a leader now of the people you were peers with a week ago.

What I am getting to here is that in any leadership role involving reports there will always be 2 key elements of management. You as the newly appointed or already appointed leader will have responsibility to 1. The business and 2. The people. This at first can seem quite difficult to be in the middle and you may not know where your loyalties are. On one hand the company is paying me so I'd better deliver, but in making that request I might be annoying or upsetting one of my reports e.g.: "can you work late and miss the big game tonight as this order is a priority and we must ship!" In this example the majority lean towards the companies requirements. Soon though there will come a big issue or decision that might force you to look at things a little differently.

To further complicate matters you don't want to be totally people sided either or it becomes a kindergarten. Very little gets done and everyone thinks you should be president. There is a happy medium here which is not easy to achieve. It needs honesty, buy in and straight talking.

For me, having the right team around you and the correct skillset is a lot like a cake. There are many ingredients in the cake to make it nice. The golden ingredients are when you understand the potential of all of your team members and unlock it. The underlying issues, concerns of individuals, their hopes, likes/dislikes strengths and weaknesses. Then you have tapped into the golden ingredients. If any one of the ingredients is not up to scratch the cake won't be as tasty as it should be. However invest time and work with your team and set clear expectations and this will look like a motivated team that surpasses all your expectations under your leadership, where you struggle to keep them motivated because they have accomplished everything you have asked of them ahead of time. Where they almost anticipate your questions and leadership style and have the answers already considered and acted upon before you even speak. Then you have unlocked the golden ingredients. Their potential to excel as part of your team which they will get from your leadership. Sounds like a dream team. Give it a go and see what happens. Even if you only unlock one of your team's potential it will feel great and benefit the team.

STORY:

There was a very pragmatic boss of mine once who had a photographic memory. He loved targets and numbers and Quarter on Quarter shipment figures and every statistic known to man was calculated. Let's just say that people for him did not figure (pardon the pun) to him as high a priority let's say, as output. This was in an Irish company and it was a very busy month for us as we used to get all the high volume of orders in that month. It was also end of quarter and used to have less available working days in that month. Needless to say my old boss wanted everything done and all the team to work. The issue here was that one of my team was getting married that weekend and had invited most of the department. Leaving us very short for help that weekend. Can you imagine me delivering that news? To say there was a mini riot would be putting it mildly. But when you are new to a role you try not to rock the boat even though your gut will tell you that this is not going to go down well (like a fart in a space suit). You also have responsibility to the people and this was one of those calls where the people would come second. All in all this was dressing up as a win/lose or a lose/lose situation. Looking back at it now though, there were so many wrongs with that call from the people responsibility side. Your team will look to you as their leader. They did not want to work this day and felt upset about having to do it. A last minute poorly planned decision had let this happen and now you're faced with this. If you agree to work, you have damaged your leadership as the team will feel you have left them down or at the very least they felt you did not represent them well. So now you are the company man and don't really have the folk's interests at heart. That is hard to recover from and hard to regain their trust.

If you don't work then your boss will be disappointed in your leadership skill and have doubts over your management capability when the going gets tough. Rock in a hard place.

Opens more doors
to development than
any other method

THE JOURNEY WITHIN

9 It can be quite easy to forget about your own development when you are busy putting out all the forest fires. It is important to keep an open mind for developing yourself. As we mature in our positions it can sometimes subconsciously feel like we have learned all we need to learn and have somehow reached a level of education that no longer requires any more development.

The reality is that we should take every opportunity to learn as much as we can all the time. It doesn't matter if the opportunity is small or big we should embrace each chance to further our knowledge. Sometimes length of service with a particular company may lead us to a false sense of being untouchable and not seeing the need for further development.

It is a bit one sided of me of course to say that you should try to use every inch of your time to further your education. Life throws challenges at us regularly and these can place huge time demands on us and development can be pushed aside for other life priorities.

An important aspect of development is knowing what areas you need to develop. This is easier said than done. One of the journeys that is closest to us but yet rarely taken is the journey within ourselves. This is where he has lost it, I hear you say. Bear with me for a while. We are all the sum of our experiences in life and we all act and behave as a direct result of this. It's easy to see the faults or areas for development in other people. The hard bit is trying to find these areas for development in ourselves. And to further complicate things what you may feel is the issue may only be a symptom or result of a deeper issue. Trying to diagnose yourself is a very difficult process and even skilled coaches rarely coach themselves.

A simple but very effective way of getting to know your areas for development is feedback. Feedback is by far the most effective way of getting to know aspects or behaviors of yours that you did not know about yourself. You can ask for feedback from your superiors, or if you are comfortable enough with asking your peers this is effective too. Feedback unfortunately can have a negative reputation and sometimes because of this people shy away from the process.

The truth is that it opens more doors for your development than any other method. Your behaviors and your actions in the workplace will form impressions and perceptions with superiors that you work with. You may not be aware of how people perceive you in the workplace. By getting feedback from a trusted source may help you to identify items that you want to improve on. Your perception at work can be the difference between promotion and no promotion. By receiving regular feedback from senior people in your organization you get valuable information from them but also you become known to them. Looking for feedback gives a very positive impression to your superiors that you are willing to, and wanting to, develop yourself.

The process is quite simple it involves you asking a superior if they would mind taking 20 minutes or half hour of their time to give you some feedback or pointers on your development. Set up a meeting and be sure to listen listen listen. Feedback should be welcomed and most of all be sure to thank the individual for taking the time to give you the feedback. It should not be argumentative or challenged. By all means seek clarification and seek examples until you are clear what is being said. When you receive your feedback it is fair to say that sometimes you may not like what you hear. Feedback is powerful and can affect you depending on your personal condition. You must "let it land," by that I mean picture it all on your chest. Some of it will soak into you and feel right and correct and some of it will feel alien and you may have reason and examples not to believe it. Do not dismiss any of it immediately. Let it stay there for a while and analyze it until you can either fully approve it or deny it. Remember that this is one person's impression of you. Depending on their level and amount of interaction with you the feedback may be very relevant or possibly distant. However it is a real live impression that someone has of you and as the old saying goes "there's no smoke without fire," maybe there are some truths in what they tell you, little nuggets or gems and the rest might be noise or might not be true. The important and most difficult thing is to be honest with yourself. It is easy to ignore all the bad and embrace the good. Try and strike a balance of good and bad feedback. Remember that essentially there is no such thing as bad feedback. I use the term only to distinguish from good. Bad feedback is a glass half empty approach. We are always learning until we die. The day we stop trying to learn or think we have learned everything we may as well die. There are only new opportunities to learn new things. Self-development is an inward journey and I have to say, is the most exciting. You don't even have to leave your sofa to take your inward journey.

Once you are working on some feedback how do you know how to make it better? One way I found very useful is to find a role model in the organization that is very good in the area you need to improve in. Guess what then? You ask them for some tips, set up a meeting and explain that you are working on some feedback and have identified them as good role models in this field. People love being told they are experts so you may be surprised how willing people are to meet you and share their experiences. Don't bombard yourself with 50 million areas for development. Take one or 2 areas every month. Be conscious and aware that you are working on these things. If you trust your boss enough tell them that you are working on this area and that you would appreciate it if they could keep an eye on your progress and include it as a discussion item maybe in your one to ones. Weight loss programs rely on the same concept that you have support from others and that they are aware that you are working towards a goal. Circle of trust and support exists and you can do the same. You can discuss with your peers and reports. Tell them you are trying to improve in this area and that you appreciate their feedback. This might sound a little crazy and indeed some folks might view this as exposing your weaknesses to others and by so doing that you may appear weak. This is a choice you must make with the people you choose. In political environments people may use this to their advantage. In my experience though, this rarely happens. The more people that know you are working on something the weaker the ammunition becomes to use against you. It's like the secret that everyone knows. It's not interesting anymore.

Let me tell you an interesting perspective on self-development that I have used over the years and to my amazement is not used as much as it should be. What I am referring to is carving your own destiny.

Now what I mean by that is taking on a certain amount of responsibility and action for what will become of you. In my experience a lot of people let themselves be part of the system (which is fine for day to day work) but this can become a problem if you expect the system to fully understand your development needs and aspirations. For example you may have an interest in a certain area of the company and wish to get there eventually. You can do 2 things. The first is you go about your daily job and hope that someday an open position comes available on the internal job postings and hopefully you will get it. The second is that you find out who is the boss of that area, book some time with them over a coffee and inform them of your interest in that area. Now a safety tip here is to ensure your boss is aware of your interest in that area, also if he or she would not approve of this action you may want to ask the boss of the desired area to keep this conversation confidential and explain your reasons. I prefer the second approach, the first approach is leaving it to the gods as it were. You have very little influence in the outcome. By taking the second approach you have established a connection with the boss of the other area. They are now fully aware of your interest and can put a face to a name for future open positions. If you are really keen then offering to work a few hours a week at your own expense in that area to get a feel for it is a great way to demonstrate your enthusiasm and dedication. It also proves that you want to work there and that you weren't just filling the boss up with great intentions.

A word of caution though some bosses may see this behavior, depending on the culture of the organization and the personality of the boss, as rogue or underhanded. To combat this as part of your development plan discussions you can inform your boss of your intentions. In that way they are kept in the loop and if the other boss was to betray your confidence your current boss would already be aware and not be blindsided (which all bosses love). Remember bosses like to be kept informed of potential embarrassing or hot topics. Always, as I am sure I have said already, try to protect them from awkward moments. Your conversations outside the circle could become awkward if your boss did not know of them. It really comes down to knowing your boss and how they will react to your future plans. Good bosses will have the conversation for you or be in attendance when you go meet the other boss to support you. Paranoid delusional types will probably excommunicate you and view the whole matter as a breach of trust. In any case you will have taken action for your development and carved out your own destiny and not waited for it to happen. Hopefully with a positive result.

A final word on self-development if I may, would be to examine your role and how long you have been doing it. Are you happy doing it for that length of time? Maybe you are? No problem. But if you are like me and sometimes feel it's time for a change then you need to give some time to the expression "it's better to burn out than to fade away." The first time I heard that was in the movie Highlander when the Kurgan said it. Although beheadings do happen in leadership, thankfully they are left to the boardroom levels now. Anyway this expression asks you a question of yourself in your role. As we stay in roles for a long time we get complacent and comfy and there is a suggestion that we lose our edge. The counter argument would say that you have acquired more knowledge in the role over the duration. In any case its worth examining if you have done all that needs to be done in a role and it's time for something new "Burn out" or you wish to stay in your role for a long time and "fade away" as it were. Both expressions are quite negative and either choice of course is fine and ultimately it is your choice but I think there is a good exercise in there now and then to examine your position and see if you can develop more by changing. I met a guy who warned me when I got the supervisor job for the first time "to be sure and only give it 5 years or you'll be dead." He was referring to the pressure of operations and feared for me jeopardizing my long life by staying there beyond the 5 years. Maybe I should have listened to him but I didn't and it's now too late for that. Damn.

STORY:

I was working in an organization where there was a need to start implementing Key Performance Indicators and weekly reports. It had been pretty much hit and miss up to now due to the business being so busy and people were overwhelmed with work. We recognized this was an area for improvement so I decided to do a little research to understand the levels people were at and what was already in place or tried before etc. I decided begin at a basic level and start trying to crawl before we could walk so to speak. I introduced it and to make a long story short it was shot down, not accepted you get my drift. A week later I was meeting with a senior manager and we got talking about this event and I said I couldn't believe they rejected it and that it was so simple. He turned to me like a wise Indian chief and said "What have you learned from this?" At first I said I don't know to which he replied "Good." This confused me more. In the end the point he was making was very valid. Always try to plan to succeed by removing every possibility that could cause your plan to fail. In this case it was an individual who was respected by the team and created a raucous. My failure here was not knowing he was the unofficial leader of the team and if I had gotten his buy-in before the team meeting he would have supported me. As soon as the team heard his condemnation of the plan the rest followed. So basically the point here is that always ask yourself what have you learned and above all keep learning and developing yourself. Everyday make yourself better and everyday take that journey within.

WHEN YOU ARE AN EMPLOYEE
ITS ALL ABOUT YOU BUT AS A
LEADER ITS ALL ABOUT THEM

MAKE THEM GROW

10

The first time I remember being asked to write a development plan for someone, I got a cold chill down my back. The expectation that I somehow had to look into my crystal ball like a mystic psychic and foresee what development this person across the table from me needed was daunting. Would it magically happen and I'd become inspired knowing exactly what to write?

The truth, thankfully, was both easier and more rewarding for everyone involved. Development plans thankfully are not in the hands of the Gods. They are a 2 way process, the plan must suit the needs of the employee and also the needs of the business. So what does that mean? Well if the employee has no interest in what you are proposing, whether it's something that they will work on or a course they could complete, then there's a pretty good chance that it won't happen. It must be linked to their interests and what motivates them. So how do you find out what interests and motivates them?

Conversation

Like I've mentioned previously it's about having a simple sit down conversation. One very important point here is to ensure that both of you are realistic about what can be achieved and/or is suitable. Cure for world hunger in Quarter 1 and world peace in Quarter 2 would be great but it's unlikely to happen. Look at your team and identify the areas that have been crying out for improvement and those that have been the 'thorn in the side' for the team too. Remember your team probably know the answers and how to fix or improve things with minimal direction from you. It just has not been structured properly for them to approach it or succeed in implementing it. There is no better project than one that makes life better or easier for everyone. Also look at the available time that your people have for these activities and ensure you agree a block of time that they can work on every day/week. If your team is really busy and time is short then both the project and the time available must match i.e. small project easy deliverables = smaller time off the core job to complete them. Of course development can be achieved through many different things and some ideas may involve the team and some maybe personal development areas for the person.

Documented Development Plan

Cross training opportunities to increase the flexibility of your team is one development that is used frequently to up-skill your team and increase flexibility e.g. so that the team has cover for when John/Mary is on vacation. No longer will that key piece of equipment, that only Joan can run and the place grinds to a halt when Joan is not in, causes everyone to become frustrated. Someone on your team may be interested in developing their skillset to get trained on that machine i.e. another skill for the toolkit. In any area for development, always keep your tasks clear and date specific i.e. the aim is to achieve training on X by end of Quarter 2. The deliverable is a signed off OJT (On Job Training) or some other proof of delivery. Deputizing for you is a good one for your next in line Supervisor/ Leader. They will get to experience the role and expectations you have of them, the pressure you are under etc.

The key thing is that the development plan works both ways. Good for you and also good for them. It's not easy but by sitting down and discussing a person's interests and plans for their future, you can cleverly link both to achieve a win-win. A point of note is that if the concept of development plans and your team development is alien to the organization start with quick wins and get people engaged and bought into the concept. Start too big and the idea may not get traction and just fall into the failed projects box.

Regular Check-in sessions

Once documented then it's not over, this is just the beginning. It is important that there are regular 'check in' sessions throughout the year to check on progress. I would suggest linking it to your one to one schedules and maybe every second or third one to one is dedicated exclusively to the development plan. That gives you 2 or 3 good sessions a year on the development plans. Depending on the complexity and type of development area you should increase the periodic reviews as you see fit.

Unfortunately there can be a sense of negativity associated with development plans. I believe that this comes from people seeing it as an extra task that really doesn't add to the bottom line and eats into their time that they don't have and some may feel what's the point anyway? That is where the leader's role comes in to engage the individual in developing, the development plan should not be underestimated and should be viewed as a formal opportunity for you to sit down and discuss with your team their own personal development. It's an opportunity for them to work on areas for improvement that may require work. If there is a master succession plan then the development plan can feed directly into that. It is important for you to know who is next in line for all key positions in your team and to use the development plan to ensure their successors are ready and properly trained should the time come. People want to know their development and where they are going. The core job is no longer sufficient to retain your employees. In fact a good development plan can contribute to employee retention, like invisible glue. So don't underestimate it, put time into it and remember it must be a 2 way thing and ensure it's followed up on.

Someone once said, "When you're an employee it's all about you, but when you become a leader it becomes all about them" You now have a different perspective for your team and this changed the focus for the development to include your team.

The other point worth clarifying, and this is worth mentioning, is that sometimes we hear the word development plans being used negatively for individuals that have maybe fallen short of a particular objective or have some behavior modifications required to improve their performance. It is because of this type of reactive development plan that the proactive and positive development plans get taken in a bad light. All tarred with the same brush as it were. I am of course referring to the positive up front identification of areas that you and your boss or you and your team agree on as areas that will benefit you or your team and the business. Not the development plans that we sometimes see partnering the disciplinary process. The significant difference is that the latter is forced on an individual with no buy-in and certainly doesn't feel positive or fun. Remember it's all about making them grow not fade. Anything that grows requires water, sunshine and a solid foundation. For humans these can be replaced by your time, support and guidance but the result is the same. Growth.

A Leader once argued with his senior mentor. The discussion was around investing in development of his people and he asked the question "what happens if we invest in our people and then they leave?" The reply was brilliant, "What happens if we don't invest and they stay?"

STORY:

This is a story from Irish Folklore that speaks of development and it goes something like this if I remember.

One day a small boy called Fionn McCumhaill was with his mother and Finnegas came by. Fionn's mother wanted Finnegas to teach Fionn about the world. Finnegas agreed.

Everyday Finnegas sat by the river teaching Fionn all he knew about the world. Then one day, a huge fish swam by. Finnegas was so excited because he was sure this was The Salmon of Knowledge. He ran to get his fishing net.

The salmon was strong. It jumped and twisted and turned in the net for a long time. Eventually Finnegas landed the fish. 'Hurray' they both cheered and Finnegas fell to the ground, exhausted. Finnegas was too tired to cook the fish so he left

Fionn in charge, with this warning 'No matter what happens - Do not eat any of the fish.'

Fionn did as he was told and cooked the fish over a big fire, turning it two or three times. After a while a bubble appeared on the side of the fish. Without thinking, Fionn burst the bubble with his thumb. 'Ouch! 'He yelled as it burnt him. He immediately put his sore thumb into his mouth to cool it and make it better.

After some time Finnegas woke up. He was very hungry and he was looking forward to having the salmon for his tea. He called Fionn who came immediately. He then noticed something strange about the boy. His eyes seemed bluer and his cheeks redder. He also looked bigger and stronger. Then Finnegas knew what had happened.

'Did you eat any of the fish?' he asked. 'No...But.... while the salmon was cooking a bubble came up on its side and I burst it with my thumb,' Fionn replied. 'Then you, and not I, are the one to get the gift of knowledge from the salmon,' Finnegas said sadly.

'You must go now, I can teach you no more - Good Luck!' From then on, if Fionn needed to know anything he just put his thumb in his mouth and he knew what to do.

What I like about this story is that

1. Fionn represents all of us who want to learn more.

2. There are always wise men around to teach you what you need to know and help is always at hand (if it isn't you are not looking hard enough)

3. Be careful of senior men following dreams of big fish

4. There is no salmon of knowledge, it is achieved through constant learning

5. Sometimes if you do stop and think and put your thumb in your mouth you might just get the answer.

6. Know when you have learned all you can learn from your leader and it's time to leave the nest and move on.

No surprises

HORNS AND HALOS

11 Nothing in the new Leader's world strikes more fear into hearts than the dreaded performance appraisal. I'm joking of course but in can be a challenging time for a new leader. Whether you are reviewing or being reviewed, the slow painful ticking of the clock towards the various completion milestones is enough to leave you with no fingernails. But help is at hand (I hope). Personally I love them and I am not alone in that thinking. It's a massive opportunity for positive experience. The clever ones would have an acronym formed by now on my last sentence M.O.P.E but rest assured it's far from that. The way we visualize things are usually worse than they really are and often all in the mind, this is one of those things.

Follow the rules and you will be fine here. Now before you slay the dragon you must first understand it. Yes, it is an annoying piece of paperwork (or nowadays online web tool that must be completed) but it is so much more than that in the great scheme of things.

The annual performance appraisal (PA) is a review process that is completed formally at the end of a year for your direct reports, and informally throughout the year. It will be an evaluation of their performance for the year under a number of headings/guidelines. Your job is to work with your employee to

- Ensure they understand their goals (at the beginning of the year if possible),

- Evaluate their performance with their input in the form of a self-appraisal

- Gather feedback on how they are getting on

- Give positive and constructive feedback.

Hopefully if done correctly you will have no issues with your team and 'all will be well in the castle'. Get it wrong however and you could have a storm that there is no scale for. This wrong doing, error or correct perception, delivered badly could stay with your team for a long time and influence their opinion of you. No pressure then.

Balance

Great, let's get started. All anyone ever wants from an appraisal is that it is fair. I'll say it again FAIR. Now a better word to digest than fair (which is used to describe 364 days out of 365 days of Irish weather) would be balanced. Now whether you despise this person or love them, your appraisal firstly, above all must be based on facts. Yes facts, no subjectivity, 'hearsay' or what your boss thinks about the individual. Facts only please ladies and gentleman. It's kind of like court of law in a way, albeit more like Judge Judy. You may not have a jury but you will have reviewers of your document namely human resources, your boss and more importantly the employee themselves. The facts must be collected by you in a way that you can stand over them if mentioned or discussed at the appraisal. Facts are undisputed which is very useful in a PA as there will be challenges and questions and general unhappiness. Although hopefully not too much of the latter. A tip here is don't reinvent the wheel. By that I mean there are data sets being collected by someone somewhere measuring you or your team's performance. You may even already have metrics that you use to measure your team. Try if possible to get individual metrics, not always easy as mostly you will be measured as a group. The individual ones are usually collected by yourself and based on individual objectives / projects that you gave individuals during the year.

Early objective setting, this is a good habit to get into. Be sure and keep a record on your computer of the 5/6 topics that you are measuring individuals on. Have a record on your computer for everyone and log it throughout the year with positives and negatives BOTH!! Not just little Santa's elves naughty lists. Build that into your calendar at the end of each day to remind you to update logs. Examples, Jim's safety suggestion today, Mary's assistance of Tim without being asked, Joes leadership in taking on and solving that problem. Specific examples are what separate ordinary PAs from Great PAs. Imagine the feeling that your boss noticed specific examples during the year of good things you did and remembered them. Wow pretty impressive. Your reputation and opinion has shot up amongst your team.

Self -Appraisal

A really powerful tool is the self-appraisal. In some companies there is a requirement for the employee to also submit a self-appraisal form. This is similar to the form that you fill out. What is great about this is that it gives the employee a chance to write down what is important to them, many people love writing about their achievements and things they want you to mention in their review. However some people may be reluctant to blow their own trumpet so ensure they get credit for work they have done. If you find yourself not as organized as you should be this self-appraisal document can be a life line to the leaders that don't collect data; a lot of the information for the PA is included in the self-appraisal. I do not encourage this behavior but sadly that happens. That is not the purpose of the self-appraisal. It is an opportunity to sit with your direct reports and go through their self-appraisal and challenge or agree with the content and also to add in achievements and challenges they faced that they have not noted. This is their opinion of themselves. Very important stuff. You need to know where they think they are and see if it tallies with where you think they are. Don't be afraid to challenge if you feel they are writing down content that will have them up for the Nobel peace prize and in reality they have missed half the year off work. In any case a level playing field has been agreed between you and your direct report and there is a greater chance of the main PA being a success now, as both of you have had your chance to discuss the self-appraisal review at a sit down session. A well rounded performance review should be the result.

Now there are millions of books on PA's and how they work. I will touch on the mechanics but not in great detail. The reason for this is that every company has its own version. So back to my earlier point of understanding the dragon. This is an important step also. Read the PA template and supporting ratings definitions. In my experience most of the PA's are linked to a rating scale. In the past a long well written essay worthy of the Pulitzer Prize was called for, happily not today... Reading the topics first. These could be safety, productivity, teamwork, leadership, working on own initiative. There are hundreds but usually 5-10 topics. These to my earlier point should form the headings for your individual files. They are usually a good spread of topics giving a pretty good snapshot. There will also usually be metrics to support these somewhere.

If someone else is collecting data, let them. Borrow it but be sure it suits the purpose. For consistency too check with your boss as to what metrics we will be drawing on for each topic. Sometimes there is a ranking process whereby everyone must be ranked 1-100 best to last. In this case the data set being used must be uniform. You can't have a set of data that cannot be compared to a neighboring team. You must compare apples with apples.

Now hopefully you will be the proud new owner of the highest performing team in the history of teams but if you are like the rest of us then you will have a mixed bag. We are all different and that is what makes this job really great. You get to work with all people of various interests and capabilities and talents. You must discover them all, what makes them tick...not (THICK) although there will be days when you will look to the heavens and wonder how bad you must have been in a previous life to deserve this. Thankfully those days are equally outweighed with good ones, not euphoric ones but happy ones too.

No Surprises

You will have to deliver some bad news sometimes in your PAs. This is fine and many people regrettably dance around issues instead of spelling it out straight to people. Improvement needed messages are fine once they are backed up with specific examples and as mentioned earlier a development plan to help them get better. It should be viewed as a way back not a slippery slope. You may have someone who is on disciplinary action and this needs to be mentioned in the review and their progress or lack of. The golden rule of the PA is NO SUPRISES. This is not a Christmas or birthday party, surprises are very bad here. Picture the scene Johnny sits down in front of you a little bit nervous and apprehensive and BAM you hit him with a 12% absenteeism figure. It would be like one of those scenes from the 1960s batman (BOOM) (KEBANG) words would appear in the room over your heads. This is the first poor Johnny has heard of this amazing statistic of yours. He will be dumb struck, upset possibly angry and you risk an embarrassing situation and possibly a walk out. Now that does not mean that you forget about this nasty statistic, it does mean that you should have been talking to him all year in your one to ones about this and helping him fix it. So again I say NO SUPRISES. If you had been sitting down with Johnny all year then he would not even flinch when you write (Johnny has had a few issues with attendance during the year, currently absenteeism at 12 % but he has been working with me to actively resolve these issues and I am happy to say has improved). The reason being that he is aware of the issues prior to the review session, it's not a surprise yet you are delivering an improvement message and not getting fireworks.

Also on the positive side you will have your high performer reviews to deal with. These believe it or not can be equally as challenging and their focus is on promotion and opportunity and this can be challenging to find in order to keep them motivated. Trying to align their talent with their interests and the business areas that may need some work or project focus can be tricky, but ultimately this is essentially the answer. The level of project complexity must match their capabilities or they may have a chance of failure and become demotivated quickly.

Personally for PA writing I prefer short sharp bullet points with a nice 5/6 line personal message, summarizing where I think the employee is at. The more factual and filled with specific examples the better it will be. This is why some leaders are terrified of PA's. They haven't done their one to ones and haven't gathered any data, they will then try and blab their way through someone's review and generally get it wrong. Beware of the POSTCARD too. When you are writing 50 reviews, there is a tendency to create a nice postcard that has the same content for everyone you are sending it to. (Weathers great wish you were here) everyone gets the same. This can be funny when the title reads Johnny and the content keeps referring to "she" and "her" or vice versa. Or the title reads Johnny and half way down reads "Shane's attention to detail is excellent" Oh the horror stories I could tell. And of course Johnny knows Shane so what do you think Johnny will do? Talk to Shane of course and maybe even for a laugh over a coffee compare their reviews word for word. I was once asked to review 120 people having only been in the company 3 months, so I ended up creating a high, middle and low performance template and applied it based on basic data available for each person, nightmare scenario and one which I do not recommend. Happily, I had no appeals to the delight or amazement of my boss.

Understand the definitions of each category in order to score fairly - exceeds expectations range. They will read like "person who constantly exceeds the goals set out for them and is consistently raising standards" This definition must apply to that person for that topic or don't use it. Read the definition and find the most suitable.

More recently PA's are linked to a rating which is linked to pay increase. Performance related pay. If you work hard you get a better rating, better rating better pay increase. Again this may not be in your organization but one item that is there is the dreaded bell curve. We have good old statistics to thank for this and of course finance. Business is not Santa's North Pole and the money is not limitless, therefore there is only so much money allocated each year for salary increases. The Bell curve quiet simply tells us that the top 5 or 10% will be the high performers the bottom 5 or 10% the low performers and the rest in the middle. You then apply your budget to this using a good old excel spreadsheet and hey presto you have divided the spoils. Typically bottom of the bell curve get zero or very little and top get more and middle get medium increases. It's a tidy system that ties money to performance and is said to encourage better performance to achieve more money, but if money isn't a motivator why do we use this system? The answer is to reward the ones who have worked hard over the ones who have just done the basic requirement. In some companies blanket payments are made without truly understanding the person's contribution to the business. This causes friction. The guy, who is out more times than he is in, is getting the same increase as you. That is why examples and well written PA's are very important. If you rate everyone as achieving and meeting the standards of the role then you can't complain that everyone is getting equal increases. So the time needs to be spent on preparing for the Pa's at review time but also throughout the year.

The document is an important one and you need to be aware of its uses. If one of your team applies for an internal job, his or her last PA will most likely be looked for by the hiring leader. If there was an issue and someone was sacked and they challenged it, the PA would be or could be looked for by the courts. It is after all a PERFORMANCE appraisal and this is a snapshot of a person's performance. That is why it needs to be truthful and contain as many facts as possible and no omissions and no cover ups and above all no surprises! Be comfortable with the expectations of yourself in this process, there is usually training available for it also. Don't go in there unprepared. Get help from experienced leaders if it's ok to do so or HR.

The session itself then, when you are ready to deliver it, go somewhere away from the main floor, be professional and set up appointments with people in their calendars. This allows them time to get ready also. Some leaders prefer the surprise attack and just collect their employees and tell them it's happening now. Thinking that there won't be any talkback or issues raised that way. Rubbish. If someone is not happy with the content of the PA then they will escalate it. Hopefully they will because if they don't it will sit with them inside and you will never understand why they are not motivated or don't trust you. If there are disagreements during the session, it is up to you to be professional and mature and listen to the employee's viewpoint. Try of course to paint a picture of where you were coming from on that point. Remember sometimes people need time to think about things and very few are accepting of perceived negative points instantly. Give them time. The session may end with you not agreeing on a point. So be it but ensure you have a follow up discussion scheduled before they leave. Be open to minor changes, phrases and wording issues. Sometimes it's the smallest thing that can upset someone. Or you may have left something out, in which case you admit it and put it in. This is not the 2 stone tablets handed down by God that can't be changed. These are important documents and they need to be right for both of you.

When you start off you may have a group or team and you think you can tell which ones may be problematic, there is always one surprise in my experience. And it's the one you least expected, prepare for all and have faith in your abilities to rectify any concerns they may have. The worst thing for you is allowing it to escalate to your boss which unfortunately says that you are not capable of handling it yourself and you might be seeing comments to that effect in your own review. It's not the end of the world and most issues can be rectified over a cup of tea and a red pen. So weigh that up when resolving disputes. Is the phrase that important to you versus having a year of a disgruntled employee?

Just remember when all is said and done out there you are all on the same team and you need these folks as motivated and ready for battle as they can be after the PA process is gone for another year.

STORY:

Performance appraisals can be a heavy subject so rather than going into my experiences I decided on a few Jokes. Apologies if I offend anyone.

1. All of this recognition stuff is ridiculous! What ever happened to just doing your job, keeping your mouth shut, taking what you are given and quitting ☺

2. Boss: You need to get better at anticipating problems

   Employee: If I could anticipate problems I would not have decided to work for you?

   Employee: You seem Angry? I did not see that coming

3. Boss: So what have you accomplished this year?

   Employee: I used my empowerment to create a new paradigm. I teamed across functional boundaries to achieve quality. I dare say I was customer focused and market driven. I proactively found excellence in the midst of chaos re-engineered my core processes and embraced change. I give you myself as the perfect employee.

   Boss: Are you being Sarcastic?

   Employee: To be honest I couldn't tell either.

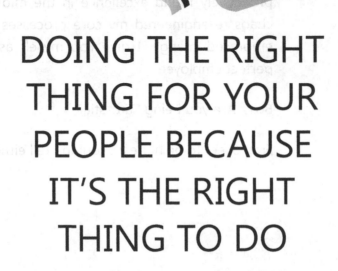

DOING THE RIGHT THING FOR YOUR PEOPLE BECAUSE IT'S THE RIGHT THING TO DO

THE NUGGET

12 You will notice by now a strong theme throughout this book, and that is that people and relationships count for number 1. I believe if you fully internalize this not just read it, that you can accomplish great things. There are Leaders I have coached close to retirement that unfortunately have still not got that important message. Now I am sure they have heard it, read it and maybe even agreed with it, but you have to wholeheartedly believe it and make decisions using it before it will be a benefit to you. You can't bluff it because you will be out of character and your team will spot that as easy as a bad neck tie. By the way if this is currently not your thinking don't panic. This has to be learned. Some people are naturals yes but I firmly believe this can be learned. Perspective plays a lot in it. Doing the right thing for your people because it's the right thing to do despite what the pressures are. That is the nugget for me. Really wholeheartedly taking into consideration people's feelings and opinions when we as leaders must make decisions. You can't please everyone is a good saying but you can sure as hell give it a try. Try for a win for the business and a win for the person.

The importance of relationships

I must admit that I have been very fortunate to get this nugget and learning early in my career. I did not always have the viewpoint that people and relationships are central. I, like most of you went through the importance of business deliverables and bottom line speeches being number 1 and was on board with them all. Sometimes unfortunately, to the detriment of my team, or relationships at work. Now I am not here skipping along the yellow brick road with Dorothy, My head is firmly screwed on and I say that a happy balance of focus between people and business metrics is not only possible but will be the difference between surviving companies and ones facing bankruptcy now and in the future. People, who are on board with your direction, involve themselves in decision making, make better suggestions, not because they have to but, because they want to. All these things paint a picture of a culture where the employee is central and cross functional relationships are extremely important. So when you are in that meeting fighting for your corner it's not the topic that should be the most important but preserving the relationships in that room. Why? Because newsflash there will be more issues the next day and the day after that and the day after that. The one constant is the people talking are the same. So there is no point in having public floggings, decapitations, putting people down, snide comments etc. As this will only damage the relationships and make fixing problems more difficult in the future.

Weighing Scale

So how do you do this on a day to day basis? Well personally I think you become a walking weighing scales, weighing up the relationship being preserved with the needs of the business and knowing when to stop for the sake of preserving the relationship. If I was to visualize this it would be a riverbank with one person on each side looking at each other with the river flowing between them. Now the river represents all the issues and events that the two people deal with as part of their daily interactions and as the saying goes "You can't step in the same river twice" meaning there is constant change at play and the river has changed by the time you step in the second time. What has not changed are the 2 people on the river banks. They are constant and important. The stuff flowing every day is just that, stuff. So put the discussion into perspective and ask is it worth upsetting someone over?

Perspectives

Now moving on slightly not only are you a weighing scale but your perspectives must change. You now need to notice people more as people. At its most basic, people are the reason the company works and that production works, they build the widgets and we all get paid. If they are not happy and feel uneasy and unwanted then you have a huge problem. If you firmly believe that people are just numbers and can be replaced then you will never get this, unless you put in a lot of hard work and behavioral change coaching. Challenge yourself every day to see the human element in what is going on, to notice the people, and ask them how they are? Get to know them. Know that one of your team has a son who has a soccer final on Saturday; ask him or her on Monday how he got on at the soccer game? If it's possible let people go home a little early for the big events. They will pay you back next week, nobody loses and you have gained leadership points. It's give and take. You will need them someday for that urgent task that might require working back an extra hour or two.

I know I mentioned this already but people arrive to work the sum total of who they are and what they are bringing with them, the mood of the day, issues at home, pressures of life etc. All this is in that meeting room too. You have to try and see the total picture. Johnny might any other day agree to your proposal but today says no and looks tired and a bit edgy. Leave him alone and come back later? Maybe an option. Here's a better one, ask him how he is doing and is he ok, that you noticed he was a little off today and can you do anything to help? At this point some of the readers of this book are shaking their heads going, "I can't do that... that fool doesn't know my company" and other such comments. However, just for one second put yourself in Johnny's shoes and imagine how nice it would be on a hectic Monday morning for someone to be that supportive. I know I would nearly be apologizing for my behavior to them, and a little embarrassed that someone had spotted me as not being professional or happy, that someone cared enough to ask, saw above the day to day stuff and saw that my well-being was more important. It is simple to do, free and takes up little time. Actually, it may cost some time if someone has a problem and you need to take the time out or reschedule a meeting, but you know what, it is worth it. People don't forget things like that. I always want to be able to meet someone 10 years later in the street and be able to have a drink or a coffee with them without trying to remember if I was a good boss to them or not. I don't want to find myself in a situation where I am trying to avoid them like the priests in the lingerie section trying to avoid detection in the Father Ted TV show.

Now don't get me wrong it is not easy to do and I know the pressures that exist in getting things done, but once you realize that those pressures are always there then it's easier to make time to notice. One thing I found really useful was understanding body language. This gives you a door sometimes and it's up to you to open it or move on to the next task. Now word of warning do not go delving into people's feelings in public meetings or public office areas, respect the person enough to take it offline to a private place. The body language sends signals out and if you start to look at people more as well as listen to key words you will start to see these signals too. There are a good few of these but for example if a person meets you in a corridor and you need to speak with them. Look at their feet quickly once they have stopped. If they are fully squared off to you toe to toe then you have their full attention, if their feet are pointing away then chances are they are not comfy talking with you or are busy and need to be somewhere else, either way it's bad and you should cut it short and book a formal appointment. Also look at your team's posture, if Jimmy is always skipping into work and now is silent and has been for a few days...hello something is up here. Actually a good business argument for all this stuff for the colder hearted business men out there is that employee well-being improves productivity and decreases absenteeism. The very first metric to go the wrong way when people are unhappy and feel they cannot get their issues resolved is the absenteeism metric. It's the only option open to people sometimes so they use it. Advice to all leaders is keep a good eye on all absenteeism and have return to work chats with your team to try and understand if there is any work related reason why they were out. Bullying and harassment all related issues sometimes result in people trying to avoid the workplace. It might have nothing to do with you or your team at all but by having return to work chats it shows that you care but also from a business point of view that you noticed they were out.

During your time as leader of the empire you will have to make difficult decisions that split you down to your moral fiber, almost like when Captain Kirk orders the new security guy to his certain death. The best you can hope for is to try and reason with people and give them all the facts. Do not retain the information for the sake of "information is power." In critical situations when you want your team to respond and to be with you, share all the facts. If you are getting pressure from upstairs then tell them, if there is nothing you can do, tell them but be sure there is nothing you can do. Ask for better suggestions or solutions from them. I can tell you now the smartest people in the world work with you, and when it comes to crisis situations Leonardo da Vinci would not get a look in with the creative minds that are at play and the solutions they come up with. Let them know your basic requirement and ask them to help with a solution. They will respect you for allowing their input, and who knows best anyways?

So in summary without flogging a dead horse try and see the human side of all situations and look beyond the basic issue or task that's on the table. Once you realize that people are the most important, you will go a long way to being a great and fair leader.

Robert Kiely

STORY:

During my time as a people leader I have had a number of issues that came across my desk. Some tragic some good news, bullying relationships. You name it. As a people leader your trust is valued and people will bring their problems to you. This one time I got approached by a girl who wanted to tell me that she was leaving. I asked her to sit down and questioned further as to why and was there anything I could do. She was very reluctant and I kept gently questioning. When she saw that she could trust me with the truth she answered that she had no friends here. At first I thought it was a trivial issue and how possibly could that lead you to quit your job. In later years I realized it is one of the top reasons why people leave there Job. It solidified my belief that people are everything. In this case there was no issue with the work or the environment. It was purely relationship or people based issue. I probably to this day have never had an easier fix to a problem. I asked the team leader to take care of the girl, brought her to lunch and eventually they were doing after work sports etc. The lesson for me was to ensure your new employees are integrated well with good mentors and people to take care of them in the initial few months because for this girl people were everything.

SO MANY LEADERS HAVE
KISSED THE BLARNEY STONE
BUT DON'T DELIVER

So many leaders have
kissed the Blarney stone
but don't deliver

WALKING THE TALK

13 Once you realize that you are the focus of your team's attention on a daily basis, it will become clear that your behavior, words and actions are and will be copied, quoted and recalled. As a leader people look to you for advice and direction. You are the go-to person for daily issues and when you really earn their trust they will come to you with their own personal issues for advice.

This chapter as the title suggests is fairly self-explanatory. If you make a promise to a team member for example, you must ensure you are true to your word. Trust is built on thousands of examples of where you deliver on your promises. This does not mean you become an errand boy or mailman. It just means if you promise you must deliver and keep people in the loop on your progress or lack of. There is nothing worse than a leader that does not deliver on his promises. Keep your progress information open also and don't think that just because it is not happening immediately that you shouldn't share your progress or update the individual.

There are so many ways in which you should walk the talk, so many leaders have "kissed the blarney stone...but don't deliver." This takes from your team's confidence in you. You may not see it but after a while your promises don't hold any water unless your team start to see you delivering on them. They don't have to be big items. I would suggest you start by taking on a relatively simple request that you can complete with minimal effort and complete it out and report out to the team or individual that you have promised. You will now have a live example of your commitment to your word. A few of these over time and your team will know you deliver on your promises.

Being known for being true to your word is like gold dust as there will be times when your team look to you to make a decision (sometimes unpopular) and your credibility could be the thing that sways opinion in your favor. Not in a conceited way but it helps your team to trust that you are making the correct decision and want their support. Put a non-credible leader in the same position and you may have a mutiny on your hands.

Your day to day actions are observed also. If you are required to wear protective equipment then you must ensure you obey all the rules. It is very hard for you to correct anyone of ill-discipline if you are an equal offender. An example of this is where a supervisor or leader has noticed that one of the team has high absenteeism and a sit down one to one is needed. Now if we picture this scenario with leader A (a leader who walks the talk) and Leader B (Leader who does not walk the talk). If you imagine the conversation that will follow between the leader and the employee who needs to be made aware of his/her absenteeism issue. Leader A will mention how important it is to be at work for your own reputation and that of the team etc. etc. Leader B will say the same thing. The reactions however from both employees will be entirely different. One employee will leave the room believing what has been said to him/her whereas the other will possibly view it as another fabrication and may not get the important performance message that they need. That is how serious it can become. You being perceived as not being true to your word is possibly the worse crime you can commit as a leader. People will not respect you and therefore will not follow you. If that seems kind of a stark realization, it's because it is a true belief of mine. Even if you are not the best leader in the world, once you are true to yourself and your team you will go far.

STORY:

I was once facing into a busy period of shipments in a company, we had fallen behind our customer demands and we were running out of days to make the product and ship it. To make matters worse this was Quarter 4 of the year which was over the holiday season and people would usually take a lot of holidays and people availability would be an issue. People feel very strongly about working Christmas and New Year's and we knew we had to try and pull out all the stops to make it happen. So essentially we were now going to have to ask people to work Christmas and New Year's away from their families and friends. Not easy but unfortunately we had fallen behind in our schedule. What we decided to do was very much endorsing the Walk the talk philosophy. The management team also signed up for positions on the assembly line and dropped all their current work and cleared all their calendars to assist in making it happen. Day shifts and Night shifts were worked. Managers and employees side by side to work to meet the customer requirements. This initiative accomplished a few things other than the basic meeting of requirements.

1. It demonstrated the seriousness / urgency of the situation

2. Showed managements willingness and commitment to the task

3. Created a respect for the management team that they were willing to sacrifice their holiday plans also and not just the employees.

We achieved our Hollywood ending and all customer orders were met ahead of time and we managed to salvage some piece of the holidays thanks to all the efforts by management walking the talk.

IT IS NOT ONE SIZE FITS ALL

THE SPOILS SHOULD BE ENJOYED

14

A very powerful tool is at your disposal that is sometimes underutilized. If you think about who you are for a second and what makes you tick (not thick). We all love a challenge to get the blood racing and enjoy the thoughts of what we can accomplish. When we finally do achieve that goal we love to be rewarded or recognized for it either publicly or privately depending on your preference.

When we as leaders look to our teams, it is very important to have a very healthy culture of give and take. By that I mean there should be a healthy 50/50 balance of requests or favors from you and your team. So for example if there was a last minute important request made to you from someone on your team to be home early that day for a birthday party or something, then someday you should be able to call the favor back. It's that I give, you give tradeoff between leaders and their teams. Or maybe it's the leader saying finish up early today guys we put a hard few days in hitting that deadline this week. It would be a reward of sorts for hard work completed.

Just trying to paint the picture of give and take. Now I am not going to go into all of the motivational theories that exist or I would need a second book but I would recommend you have a look at them as it helps to have an understanding. They may partially be applicable or you may find yourself having a piece from one or a piece from another. The important thing to remember about motivational theory is that it is not one size fits all. If we were that easy to understand as human beings leadership would be easy. But most people do love a reward at the end of our projects or our hard work. Your job as a leader is to instil it as part of the day to day culture and behavior. If it is viewed as the norm that hard work gets rewarded in your team, it creates a motivated environment that feeds more engagement.

The key thing about reward and recognition is to notice where you can apply it and also to know what level is appropriate. Every day you need to train yourself to notice opportunities for recognition. Sometimes I heard leaders say "but there wasn't anything really worth recognizing there." I say you're not looking hard enough. It's easy to spot the fabulous project that saves a bucket of money. It takes a trained eye to spot the subtle things like good teamwork, good safety practices and 100% attendance records. Start using your metrics and your KPI's (key performance indicators) to plot some trends. Maybe there has been a prolonged performance result. It might be no safety incidents in Quarter 1, it might be zero absence days by the team. The really experienced leaders target areas of improvement and lay down a challenge with the promise of recognition if improvement is delivered. Remember what I said about promises, they must be kept. The level of reward is important too or else the whole effort can be undermined and the positivity lost. In fact get it wrong and it can be counterproductive I.e. comments like "we worked really hard on this and this is all we get?" The reward must match the achievement. Now I am not saying that we should all get Ferrari's if we achieve a few million savings. Equally though we should not get a supermarket voucher for 20 Euros/Dollars/Pounds. Equally and just as importantly to be thanked or mentioned in a meeting or efforts acknowledged at public communications can also be enough. The balance is important. A good leader never takes credit for others work, they let the world know who did all the work.

Most companies will already have an inbuilt reward and recognition system. A lot I have witnessed are not being used to their full potential. They are not integrated into the daily work lives of your team. Also there sometimes are awards for different things like innovation or cost savings. Some of these in big corporations allow people to travel to an awards ceremony abroad. However very few people in my experience know the deadline dates for submissions and the opportunity passes. A true nausea moment for me is when I hear about a project that won the award and I know that another leader's project would have knocked the socks off the winner but it was never submitted. Not blaming anyone but like I said awards need to be understood and marked in your calendars so submission dates are not missed. This says a lot about you as a leader, you are looking out for opportunities for your team to be rewarded on the biggest stage possible within your company. Not a lot of leaders do that or have time for that. My advice is make time. The skeptics may say it is just a piece of glass but believe me when I say that your credibility as a people leader and a giver of rewards will have received a major boost.

Take a look at what is on offer in terms of the reward systems that are in place. See if they can work for you. Try and link existing rewards to performance and try and draw up some rough criteria for each category to ensure consistency. An example would be the gold, silver and bronze system. Each color has a criteria for $ savings maybe or another criteria and a defined amount of money value for the recipient. Certain project types for example could then be linked to a certain level of reward. In lean Six Sigma a lower level project red/yellow belt might get the entry level reward, or a black belt project might achieve the highest reward and maybe a submission for a global award. Another very clever system I saw was a well thought out budget of a small amount of money each month. Random items were purchased and placed in a drawer with a key held by the leader. Anytime a team member carried out a small act they were rewarded by being allowed to select an item. Examples were working back a few minutes to ensure a good handover, or helping out a colleague. I particularly like this one as it not only rewards people for small acts of kindness but starts a culture of reward and recognition which is very powerful and clears the way for project based R&R that we have spoken about. It also creates a culture of positive reinforcement when trying to change poor behaviors. If you want certain behaviors to be the norm then by rewarding publicly the person carries out the positive behavior. Well done for wearing those safety glasses for example. In my experience it's up to you to make it happen and start rewarding performance. You will be glad you did. Work environments can be hard work so when the opportunity arises the spoils should be enjoyed.

STORY:

One of my favorite times was when we were trying to introduce a new safety culture which was struggling. People did not view it as important. We had the best teams delivering training and information on the program but it still wasn't gathering any traction. I decided to announce one day that I was going to use one aspect of the program which was "early identification of Hazards" as a KPI. The team that posted the most early safety interventions that month I would take out to dinner. The result was slow at first but quickly gathered momentum and competition from rival shifts kicked in. The result was great and people were competing to have the safest workplace and before long it was a regular KPI (key performance indicator). So with a little thought and vision you can motivate your team in all areas. And yes we had a great night out on the town as our reward. And we enjoyed the spoils of our success.

A GOOD SCHEDULE LEADS
TO AN ORGANISED TEAM

TIME IS PRECIOUS

15 As a leader one thing you will never have enough of is time. There will never seem to be enough hours in the day or days in the week to get it all done. This can be incredibly stressful for a leader over a sustained period. If you find yourself in this situation you need to deal with it straight away and not let it control you or your day. It's like an untamed animal that will eat you alive unless you house train it.

A lot of people develop their own systems of managing time, and believe me there are some excellent home grown systems out there. My suggestion is to sign up for one of them and you will see the mechanics of it. They all involve the prioritization of items. Some items are brought to your attention some are part of your day to day work. The systems try and get you to prioritize the minutes and seconds in your day to firstly achieve the important day to day stuff. If you don't keep the ship afloat by attending to the day to day stuff first then the ship will sink. Structure your day with the core activities. This forms the shell of your day. You then sequence the rest of your tasks in order of importance and fill in the available time gaps. In that way you have a plan for your day. It is then important to close it out and carry over any new meetings or unfinished work so you can reschedule.

They say the early bird catches the worm, personally I used to ensure I arrived early to have the best possible plan made out before my day officially started. That gave me the best chance of success for that day. Now a point of note as we are all human and things happen during the day to distract us or derail us. No matter what happens in any given day be sure to open your plan in the morning and close out your plan in the evening. There will be days when you say I will do it tomorrow, but this only lets the chaos back into your day. The difference between an effective leader and an ineffective leader can mean that personal organizational capability. Be ruthless with your time. Schedule everything to allow proper time and respect to it. Don't entertain 'drop in's' (too much) I understand there are times when it is necessary. Look to your existing meeting forums and see if there is a suitable time to deal with the concern. However if someone turns up at your door in tears you don't ask them to schedule some time on your calendar next week. (People first remember) You will know the drop-ins that can be scheduled and the ones that can't. You may have to sacrifice some of your time for drop-ins which you need to reschedule later and include as an uncompleted item in your closing plan. Drop-ins can be a useful tool for gathering information that you may not have been aware of. And of course always have an open door policy for your team. How do I do both? I hear you say. You will find the majority of drop-ins are not your direct reports but other departments. If it is the case that you have an excessive amount of drop ins from your direct team you might want to look at the communication channels that are available to your team for information up and information down. If they feel a need to be dropping in on you then they are not getting the information that they need from the morning meetings or one to ones. Maybe look at meeting agendas to include the stuff they want to know about or have an AOB (any other business) section at the end of your meetings to give opportunity to ask those questions. In that way you have less drop-ins.

One very important thing which may sound strange is to be sure to schedule time for yourself to reflect. Now you don't have to take the pose of Rodin's sculpture The Thinker, but make time for yourself. You are the leader, leaders look ahead to see the potential rocks that could sink the ship. You are in the crow's nest. Reflect on what's going good and what's not so good. Are you on track to where you said you would be? Are the Objectives on track? Are development plans going well? Is there a need to change or tweak anything? Is your vision communicated clearly and still relevant? (Business can change and it's important that you stay current) Will you be able to kick back like Hannibal in the A-Team and say "I love it when a plan comes together" or will it be more Leonardo di Caprio in the Titanic? There are things to think about is my point here and they won't happen on their own. You can drive your train or be a passenger on it. Taking the time to think about these things is important. Now any good leader will know there is a future to consider too so be sure to think about the future too. Where is the larger company going? How can your team align with that? For example if the company is restructuring, then have a restructuring plan ready before it's asked for. No point in hiring if there are redundancy's on the way. I know these are obvious examples but align with the future of the company. Maybe you have ideas, suggestions things you saw work somewhere else. Don't be afraid to use those ideas. So make time for 'you' in your schedule.

A good schedule leads to an organized team and an organized perception of you as a leader. Appointments are kept, tasks are completed on time and a professional way of doing things will surround you and it's not that hard to do once you embrace the correct system for you. Ensure though that you embrace some system.

STORY:

I remember a chaotic time when I was a manager when all sorts of things would hit me, meetings I had to go to and conversations that had to be cut short with half promises to catch up later (which never happened). Important insights I never had time to look for. Guidance I should have been looking for and never did. One to Ones that I had to cancel because there was not enough time and something was perceived as more important. Of course at this stage I had no system or calendar, I saw it as a lot of extra work and how could I do it anyways because I had no time to do my day to day stuff let alone take on a calendar. It all got to me one day and I decided to take on a time management course. It was the best thing I could have done. Sometimes we need to learn new things despite how old or effective we think we are. I had no shame in thinking I needed help (which is a good mindset to have). A very basic system had me recovered and a lot more effective as a result. Now I had time to do stuff and plan and speak with people. It was like a weight had been lifted. Probably the starkest realization I had was how much time was actually available in a day. When we think of tasks sometimes we see them as huge time eaters but in actual fact it is maybe 20 minutes. I found I had extra time left. And as I got better at using the calendar I was able to book time with myself or set up meetings with myself to review data or strategic thinking etc. So I highly recommend you getting some professional help or course. You don't have to spend a fortune either. Most people today have a system so ask them to show it to you and how it works for them.

NOBODY GIVES THANKS FOR
THE ELECTRICITY BEING ON

ELECTRICITY

16 A lot of books I have read are great at giving the theory and to be fair there is always a level of theory that needs to be understood. However I have tried in this book to be as practical as possible in my approach.

There are some areas of leadership that can be pricklier than others. These are a bit like electricity. When running well nobody notices or gives thanks, However when they are not running well everyone is up in arms and this can cause some problems. Nobody gives thanks for the electricity being ON, maybe we should.

On the same note, if there was one particular area that can spark disputes and hours of human resource management meetings and bitter faces, would be the management of payroll and allocation of holidays. Let's deal with the payroll option first. The first thing to realize is that even if this is managed impeccably then it is just viewed as a normal expectation. Your staff don't understand how complicated it is or all the behind the scenes activities that happen to enable a perfect pay slip. It is just an expected outcome. And you as a customer shopping on Saturday have the same expectation from a product or service. We don't really care how it got there or how long it took to manufacture and deliver. However if we get it wrong we can create an upset or distraught employee unnecessarily and damage relationships. They may feel demotivated etc. Get the timing wrong with the pay at a critical time for them e.g.: right before their holiday and you have a seriously annoyed employee. A similar level of annoyance is felt when employees are not given what they perceive as their rights to holidays and holiday pay.

So how do we fix it? Well, like all successful approaches a good system helps you to ensure consistency in your approach. Many places will have a system for payroll and deadlines for data to be submitted or entered. These submissions are very important and mark your calendar appointments to remind you to review, approve and submit these always on time. Top Priority. This is people's livelihood we are messing with here. Equally if there are errors even through no fault of yours treat these issues as top priority and involve the individuals and provide regular updates and most of all apologize for the error. These are ticking time bombs if not dealt with directly. Don't put them off or deprioritize them. Know this, there is nothing else going on mentally with the affected employee until they feel their issue is being worked on or resolved. They won't exactly be motivated now will they? By taking it on yourself you are demonstrating indirectly that you see it as very important and they will be grateful for this and relax more quickly. If you can arrange a reimbursement for them within the week that would be great if not then ensure it is included in next week's payroll. The main things are involve them and assure them you are working on the issue. Don't fob it off or you will regret it, maybe not today or tomorrow but the wheel always turns. People understand that mistakes can happen, but they demand a level of urgency equivalent to the level of their worth. If you don't take it on as urgent or put something else ahead of their issue you are saying they are not important.

In terms of holidays, the fix here is also having a good system but unfortunately a good system is not enough on its own. You need the team's involvement for a truly great system. The best approach is to let them organize their own holidays. This might sound scary but they understand the business as well as you and they know each other's skill sets needed to make the day to day event happen. You set the outlying rule i.e.: only one person allowed off per day for example. They set up a public board or spreadsheet that all can see including yourself and then you have a hassle free solution. If you are not comfortable with this or if the team is not developed enough to take this on effectively then you can manage them with a form system where people apply for their holidays and these get approved by you and you inform them yes or no. You will need to consider your team's strength and a bit of planning for that day in advance. Who is covering for Mary or Johnny on that day? Is the cover person off that day? What activity is on that day etc.? Try and visualize the day. Even this self-managed system requires some public rules to be set out by you. Notice period, quantity allowed off at any one time, where it is logged. Your approach to last minute requests is also important. Some people think they can walk up 5 minutes before business day ends and request the following day off. This behavior should be politely discouraged because if tolerated can create chaos and also if tolerated from only certain individuals can create a perception of favoritism. Just remember we all miss electricity when the lights go out!

STORY:

I have had so many payroll and holiday related incidents in my career but one sticks out more than others in my memory. Probably because it involved both holidays and payroll on a large scale. So we had a benefit that we used to extend to the employees that you don't see too often anymore called "holiday pay". It worked like this. You applied for your holiday pay which essentially pulled in your normal pay to be paid early to enable you to have your money before you left on your holidays. So you would get an additional 2 weeks earlier than they were normally due. A pay advance if you will. To make matters worse we operated a shutdown whereby everyone took the same calendar 2 weeks off for their summer vacation. Needless to say we had a problem and the holiday pay did not go through. I did not know this at this point. I was walking the lines one morning when I was approached by one individual then 2 then 3 and before I knew it there were about 10 people around me screaming at me. "How would they pay for their hotels and feed their families, this is a disgrace etc." I tried to calm everyone down and said I will follow up with payroll. As I was walking up to them I recalled the sense of genuine fear and disgust in their eyes and voices. All excited looking forward to their holidays and we had ruined it. Despite any recovery we might do we had already lost. This would not be forgotten and would damage the company reputation. Fortunately the payroll group went into an emergency plan and started issuing checks and I allowed people to go the banks. Unfortunately the banks were insisting on 3 days clearance but at least it was better than having nothing in the accounts. So in the end some agreed to the bank cheque option and some to wait for next payroll run. But the chaos and time invested that day by myself and payroll team all over a box that wasn't ticked on a computer was unbelievable. But 9 times out of 10 the system worked flawlessly a bit like electricity but only when it's gone do you realize. We take it for granted. So to this day I carefully look at holiday and payroll process to ensure I never have that experience again.

SO LISTEN I MEAN

REALLY LISTEN

DIVIDE & CONQUER

17   Despite your unrivalled popularity as a leader, there will be times when issues can get away from you, become larger than expected and the main talking point of your team. Sometimes these talking points can boil over and lead to a march into your office by a group or worse still an ambush in a corridor.

To a new supervisor or leader being put on the spot by a group of unhappy individuals, can be a daunting event. The trick is obviously to not let it get to boiling point by ensuring that your communication channels are open and also your thermometers are intact to test the current temperature of your team. These are venting channels or forums that you must ensure that you have in place for folks to frequently air their concerns or opinions. The art of listening is the best skill to have. By doing so you avoid the boiling kettle issue that we are talking about now. If you do not have one to ones or informal chats with your team then prepare yourself for lots of boiling kettles. Remember though that boiling kettles can also make tea. Turn a disadvantage into an advantage whenever you can. You may not always see the advantage but over time you will learn to spot them and recognize them.

So in the situation where we are confronted with a group of people. As the title of this chapter suggests, divide and conquer. Not in a medieval sense with swords and mindless violence but in a way that you can manage the situation first then the core issue. As an additional thought the core issue may not always be immediately apparent. The issue itself might be small but it is the "straw that broke the camel's back" or "the last straw." The issue could also be as a result of second or third hand information.

Listen

The first thing to do is to listen to the issue to contain the situation which is essentially a desire to be heard. So listen. I mean really listen. No interruptions! Let them speak but not intimidate you. It's important not to compromise respect and that applies to you also. If you feel you are being bullied simply listen to the issue and reply that you will get back to each of them individually. Taking on a group takes training and a lot of comfort in your job and your own skin. I would not recommend it if you are new to your role. Use paraphrasing to call back the issue and clarify it to them as a group before you disband them. I would also suggest you try and calm them down before they leave. If they are not feeling listened to or understood they may darken the door of your boss with their problem which only reflects bad on you as a leader (not being able to solve it on your own, still needing to have your hand held). So calm them down reassure them that you can do all you can on this issue for them. Check for signs of belief in their body language. Tightened faces are bad. Make lots of eye contact with all members. Take notice of sitting and standing positions. If you are sitting you appear vulnerable to them which is ok as you do not wish them to feel intimidated. However if they have crossed the respect line you can always stand up.

Walk the Talk

Now the important bit, empty promises are dangerous and remembered. People prefer honesty even if its bad news and you cannot help them and their current issue. They need to understand that you have done all you can, share the steps that you are going to take and later have taken to help them and the roadblock or policy that may exist. Or sometimes it's a decision you have made. Decisions like everything else can be good or bad. Rare is it 100% correct with no implications. Business is tough and sometimes people get hurt. Your job is to ensure you minimize casualties. People are number 1. By sharing what you have done and why you have done it gives your team a viewpoint that they may not have considered or have had access to before. If they have they will at the very least know the reason why you made your decision. If you're not mature in your role you will find that sometimes it's better to get a few opinions on a decision before you go public. Seek out a wise peer someone you can trust that won't use it against you. Seek advice amongst your direct reports, pitch the problem to them and ask them for their opinions. When I was starting out this was a taboo thing to do. They called it giving up your leadership. In my opinion two heads are better than one. Also if your team has provided you with a workable solution there is 100% certainty that they are bought into it being a success. Of course if you are spineless and don't make any decisions yourself you will appear to be a figure head with no real decision making ability and you will lose the respect of your team.

So in terms of the group listen to them commit to getting back to them individually, disband the group and most importantly keep your promise to follow up. If it is taking more than a day keep them informed of your progress, yes! All of them individually. (As you get to know them better you can update them as a group) This will demonstrate your commitment to them and also what you are made of in times of their needs. They depend on you to help them and sort things out. So you will be judged on how well you deliver. Not on the outcome but the lengths you went to try and solve it. Remember you are their leader and leaders lead in good and in bad times and always try to clear away the rocks so the ship won't crash. Be honest with them and you will preserve your leadership and earn their deepened respect.

STORY:

I worked once with a cross functional team and we were all the same level in the organization. Politics was ripe in this organization and unfortunately I and he did not see eye to eye. It started with small things like actions not being completed on time and no reasons given and escalated one day to a full blow up in a meeting with others present. The risk here was that he may attract favor amongst the team and increase his following. I had to take action and opted to request a separate chat in front of the team to resolve our differences. We sat down and I highlighted, respect issues and just what I thought of his behavior. He had his moment of protest and this went on for a while. Eventually we said at the very least we professionally respect each other even if we were never going to be best friends. I was approached after the meeting by another attendee and they complimented me on how I handled the situation which confirmed to me that I at least had not lost the respect of the group which I was happy to hear. So happy endings all around. But if I had chosen to go blow for blow in front of the team I would surely have lost the respect of the team. Also in those situations sides can begin to form and end up splitting the team. Sometimes doing what feels natural (in this case going blow for blow) is not always the correct way to respond. So in this case dividing and conquering tactic worked for me.

INTEGRATE THE PEOPLE

BOAT WITH ROTTEN WOOD

18 Throughout your time as leaders you will be trying to find the perfect balance for your organization. At times you will feel like you are a Swiss watchmaker trying to keep all the pieces moving and trying to make the perfect timepiece. Maybe it was just me but every time I felt I was close to the perfect structure or organization invariably it changed and set me back. This can be very frustrating being close to the finished article but never quite getting there. It's like the perfect order of things or an organized balance in the force. You think your staff are happy, motivated and your organization runs like clockwork. Even the unforeseen problems are easily dealt with. Your life as a leader has become as effortless as breathing.

Trust your team

Try and visualize the various aspects of your leadership role, and see the meetings, metrics escalations etc. View it all as a boat. With each multiple part as a piece of the boat and you feel that you have now mastered them all and at last the boat assembly is now complete. Even though it feels good and you have mastered the boat construction, remember remember remember that focusing on the visual components of the boat you are building, you are only looking at what you can see and not what you can feel. You must listen and trust your people and what they are interested in, their development and their concerns, their futures. Unless you integrate the people in your boat you will be left with a beautiful looking boat with rotten wood. A boat with rotten wood. What I mean by that is that it's totally useless. It's great to look at but only impressing the few. As we all know after a while the boat will break up and sink. Your people as I have said are the heart and strength of your boat, without them the structure is weak and breakable. Not all of us are using all our senses all the time. If you are not and focus only on your physical pieces and ignore your people, you will have created an effective, hollow work of art that looks good on the surface but is hollow at the core only those with true vision can see what lies ahead. Now don't get me wrong good systems and processes enable an effective ship but the success factor is when you hit troubled waters. Will the boat survive the rough waters or break up. Too much human glue or depending on people is going too far the other direction. A healthy balance of Good people, good systems and processes is the best way forward. Without it you will effectively have a boat with rotten wood.

STORY:

I remember a time when I was in charge of an assembly line high volume. The work was mundane enough and the team were relatively new. One brave employee disclosed to me that people weren't happy but we couldn't put our finger on the reason or rational for it. Nothing had changed productivity was good targets were being met. It puzzled me for a while and I had a number of follow up chats with the person and eventually one day he maybe grew tired of my probing questions to get to the bottom of it. Even then I saw the importance of having a happy workforce. He turned suddenly and was obviously frustrated with me and said "I don't know what's wrong with them, maybe they are just bored!!!" and in that instant a light came on in my head. "That's it "I said. And that was exactly it. We had formed a new team but there was no synergy or fun between them. I immediately singled out the appropriate candidate and asked that we get some progressive games going. Fantasy football, horse racing sweeps on big race days, raffles etc. He had a talent for it and the effect was noticeable and after a few weeks I called the guy back in again and asked him had we succeeded and he smiled and claimed he had fixed the problem and wanted to take credit. I smiled back and said "you're right you did fix it."